Sunday and Holyday Liturgies
Cycle C

Colm Murphy ofm.conv

Listen and Proclaim Publications

Fr Colm ofm.conv. is the author of First Steps in Contemplative Prayer and Sunday and Holyday Liturgies (Cycle A). He has been contributing sermon outlines to Clergy Review, the Universe and Intercom for many years. He studied theology at Oxford University and pastoral theology in Brazil, England and Wales. He now promotes Base Communities.

Published by
Listen and Proclaim Publications
16 Burgate, South Shore,
Blackpool FY4 2QH

Copyright ©Listen and Proclaim Publications
ISBN 978-0-9560399-1-0

Contents

	Page
Introduction	1-3
Preface	5
Season of Advent	7-14
Season of Christmas	15-22
Season of Lent	23-36
Season of Easter	37-56
Season of Ordinary Time	57-120
Feast Days	123-130

Introduction

1. Children and young people today are competitive. They are not inclined to be resigned and passive. They want to play an active part in their human and Christian development. They have a growing awareness of their human, democratic and Christian rights as well as their responsibilities. The priority of young people has to do with becoming more human and personal. Here the church has to watch its body language. It has to present Jesus Christ and the church itself as having a mission to set the downtrodden free from every oppressive force. The modern social and scientific revolutions are partly behind our modern self-understanding.

2. It was not, and is not, Jesus' priority to go about boasting that he was God. Jesus wants us to believe in his Incarnation in practice as well as in theory. His humanity is not something that we can forget about as soon as we find his divinity. It is not possible to bypass his humanity because, as we'll see shortly, Jesus actually gives us himself. And that includes his humanity. When we believe in the Incarnation, we also have to believe in Jesus' historical project to set the downtrodden free, and not just on paper! In real life!

Jesus' priority has to do with sharing his fully liberated, mature and risen humanity. He wants us to be mature human beings. It is by sharing in Jesus' struggle to build a more human and liberated world that we begin to meet God, because the God of Jesus Christ is someone who gives life here and now.

"Faith must be nurtured and protected, but within real life. In today's world, a strong faith can only develop within the public square, in a challenging debate and dialogue with the realities of life and progress, with the physical and human sciences, and indeed with the concrete realities and experiences of the individuals and the interactions of individuals who make up society" (Diarmuid Martin, Archbishop of Dublin, Lecture 2009).

How do we know that Jesus was (and is) divine as well as human? He shows us as well as telling us. At one point in the gospel drama, St John the Baptist sent messengers to Jesus to ask if he (Jesus) was the Messiah. Jesus replied: "Go back and tell what you have heard and seen. The blind see, the lame walk and the poor have the Gospel preached to them".

" I am struck by the insecurity in the lives of some people that their religious formation has engendered, something that I find hard to reconcile with the freedom Christian belief should bring"(Archbishop Diarmuid Martin). The church needs the Old Testament and it needs human reason to tell us something about the Christian God. But we tend to forget that the knowledge that comes from the Old Testament and human reason is an impersonal knowledge of God - from outside.

Then we start to think, mistakenly, that we have a contract with God. He gives us the commandments and we have to worry about keeping them. After a time this can become a burden. We start to worry about our performance. We then have less and less time to evangelise the poor. And to let the poor evangelise us.

Finally, we start to think of the Christian God as a sort of cosmic Policeman who punishes sinners! One Catholic journalist, writing in The Daily Mail recently, said: "As a Catholic, I carry 2,000 years of guilt!" At this point we need to go back to Jesus Christ, the man from Galilee, and try to remember that he has a mother and a grandmother. Anybody who has a grandmother is definitely human! When Jesus talks about man or God he is talking from the inside. He is talking from personal experience. St John says: "No one can come to the Father except through me... he who sees me sees the Father". "No one has ever seen God. It is the Son who is nearest to the Father's heart who has revealed him".

Now Jesus is not under any spell. He is not under the spell of the Old Testament, and he is not under the spell of human reason – though he respects both as I said above. Jesus is free to give us a new commandment. A new commandment of love. "A new commandment I give you, that you love one another as I have loved you". This means that all the old commandments (including the 10 commandments), have to be reinterpreted in the light of Jesus' new commandment. And the same is true for human reason. Jesus makes possible a more human and personal way of life. The relocation of the sacred.

When it comes to communicating the Christian faith today our schools seem to be lacking in confidence. In fact none of us seem to stride out boldly like David when he went out alone to face the pagan Goliath. The church is on its way to putting this right. But there is no room for complacency. One of the major reasons for this lack of confidence has to do with the fact that the Christian God has "Moved his abode from the Temple, to the body of Jesus" (Duquoc - one of the leading French theologians today). St Paul tells us that Jesus now shares the sacred with the Christian community, "You are the Temple of God".

In the old days the sacred could be found in the heavens, "The heavens proclaim the glory of God". The sacred could also be found in the Temple, the Cathedral, the King and so on. "God is now found in the human person and the human community" (Fr. Juan Louis Segundo, S.J.). He comes to us in a human way. He gives himself in a human way. He gives himself completely. He shows us how to give ourselves completely. My impression is that this is an exhaustible mine, for our modern struggles with belief in the sacred, human rights, justice and peace, freedom, equality, community, family and so on.

In speaking to the Father, Jesus says: "The glory that you have given me, I have given to them... I have loved them as much as you loved me".

The coming of Jesus is always a joyful human and Christian *adventure*. This is the way that the Prophet Isaiah sees it: "Arise shine out, for your light has come. The glory of the Lord is rising on you, though night still covers the earth. The nations come to your light, and kings to your dawning brightness. The riches of the sea will flow to you, the wealth of the nations come to you. Everyone in Sheba will come, bringing gold and incense and singing the praises of the Lord" (60, 1-6).

Preface

I am sure that many of you have been attracted to the use of the Liturgical Publication by Father Colm Murphy ofm.conv. in previous years. I am very happy to write this Preface to the homilies for the 'Liturgies of Sunday and Holydays in Cycle C' - aware that many people, both priests and teachers, will be struggling week by week to find something 'new' to say.

Father Colm does not so much as try to say something 'new' each week, but rather he presents his material in a very attractive way for those who will be hoping to hand on something 'new', sharing his own insights as a priest.

I mention those who might use this book as being both 'priests' and 'teachers'. I myself at one stage was both a priest and a teacher in a State school and I appreciate the challenge faced by both types of people. That challenge is outlined in the introduction to the sermons where there are valuable indications as to the 'relocation of the sacred'. Mention is made of a lack of confidence in our schools and in communicating the Christian faith today.

I am sure that the words of these homilies will, indeed, help preachers and teachers, as well as listeners, make the Gospel their own and hand them on in their everyday lives.

We all must be fully aware of that 'exalted vocation' of which the late Pope John Paul II wrote. What better way of living out our exalted vocation than through the mission of preaching and teaching that living Gospel of Jesus Christ - stimulating others and sharing with them - perhaps our weekend liturgies or in a classroom day by day.

+Keith Patrick Cardinal O'Brien
Archbishop of St Andrews and Edinburgh

June 2009

The Season of Advent
He comes in a hidden way

1st Sunday in Advent
Stay awake, praying at all times
Luke 21: 25-28, 34-36

St Luke is talking here about the final coming of Jesus. Western people today will think that this looks menacing, while St Luke is thinking of Jesus' mission to liberate, redeem and save his people.

The human community is sometimes controlled by a small group of very rich and powerful people who try to impose their values (or lack of values) on the rest of the community and especially on the poor. Some religious communities suffer a similar temptation. Building a more human community on justice and love is usually not the priority of the high command in the city. The danger is that the poor will try to escape the powers that be with drink, drugs, endless holidays, lotteries and so on.

St Luke is also aware that a small group of disciples of Jesus will be tempted to believe that they should be in charge of the church, because the ordinary folk cannot be trusted with a creative role in the church. Meanwhile, it is the poor who suffer.

It is a mistake to think that Jesus is a detached, diplomatic and professional Messiah who hates to disturb the comfort zone of the powerful! Now we can begin to see why St Luke is talking here of cosmic upheavals. Jesus takes the oppression of the poor as a personal insult. The cosmic upheavals mentioned here are like an echo of the original social and religious upheaval that happened when Moses led the Chosen People from slavery in Egypt to freedom in the Promised Land.

At Jesus' second coming the foundation of the old oppressive order is shaken. Jesus comes to put an end to the oppression of the poor. We have to suspect that there is a warning here for the blind oppressive forces that are still at work in the world. They need to repent while they have time. Jesus is a personal Messiah, not a professional one.

Rich and poor are solemnly advised to "watch and pray". Jesus is at work in the human community. It is by listening to the word of Jesus that the disciples can read correctly the social, political, economic and religious signs of the times. That is, what the Spirit of Jesus is saying to the church and the world.

A disciple needs to be aware that Jesus comes in a hidden way. Hidden from anybody who does not listen (with the community) to the word of Jesus. His first coming, as a child in a manger, was celebrated only by Mary, Joseph and the shepherds and the Wise Men later. The presence of Jesus in the poor can easily be missed. Even by members of the church.

Discussion Questions:

Does Jesus come in a hidden way today?

What does St Luke mean by "watch and pray"?

Are there any oppressive forces at work in the secular city today?

Why does Jesus come "with great power and glory"?

Are we happy with the church's preparation for the Nativity?

Does St Luke reassure the poor that their oppression is coming to an end?

What is St Luke saying to the high command in the secular city today?

What sort of people indulge in escapist stuff today? Rich or poor?

How are we preparing for the coming of Jesus?

2nd Sunday of Advent
All mankind shall see the salvation of God
Luke 3: 1-6

St Luke positions the Advent of Jesus within the political world of the Roman Empire. He then goes on to say that "All flesh shall see the salvation of God". But it begins in the wilderness. A long way from the holy city (Jerusalem) and the pagan city (Rome).

What is different about the desert is that it may have a few camel tracks, but no motorways. This means that a person or a community have to find new pathways. This is especially relevant for the church today. Will it take the risk of searching for new pathways, or hold grimly to the old?

St Luke says that we have to "Watch and pray". Why? Because our class, our tribe, our city will tend to put us to sleep. Or at least to become professional, to save energy. Fr. Flor McCarthy gives us an excellent picture of what can happen to the professional man or woman. 'Habit is a scourge which paralyzes and in the end snuffs out life. We need to be provoked, to be goaded from time to time like oxen. We make a beaten track for ourselves. Woe to the person who tries to disturb us! How worn and dusty are the highways of life. How deep the ruts of tradition and conformity. We forget that we once had dreams. We sit in our armchairs practising idle and musty virtues, passing judgement on everything and everybody'

'It can easily happen that we become Christian by habit only. Over the years the dust of routine has been falling silently and secretly. We are only going over the motions, taking part in rituals that have lost all freshness and meaning. We don't hear the gospel any more'.

St Luke is aware that, because Jesus' gospel is a universal gospel of justice and love, this would mean that "Jesus himself and his disciples would come into conflict with the forces that control the political and religious systems of Jerusalem and Rome' (La Verdiere).

St Luke talks of repentance here. The poor need some sort of conversion, because they tend to fall under the spell of the city, and of the people who control the city. The focus of the city today is on the competitive individual, who takes care of himself, and does not worry too much about the community.

However, it is usually the man or woman who controls the city that needs to repent when he hears the word of Jesus.

Usually, the word of Jesus does not produce a rich harvest today until it passes through the humanity of an active local Christian community that makes the gospel its own, in a personal way.

Discussion Questions

What is so special about the wilderness?

Should the church today keep to the well-beaten paths?

Why does the Prophet, John the Baptist, go to the wilderness?

Does the city ever have crooked ways?

Why does St Luke talk so much about Rome and its rulers?

How can Jesus make the crooked way straight?

How can we make the crooked ways straight today?

Why do the poor need some sort of conversion?

Do the rich have to repent?

Do the rich and poor need the help of the local Christian community to get involved in repentance?

3rd Sunday in Advent
Baptism and Social Justice
Luke 3: 10-18

John the Baptist was a Prophet, but he lived at a time when cult, law and apocalyptic stuff had supplanted prophesy. This meant that there was nobody to defend the cause of the poor and downtrodden. Being an austere desert man, John tended to think in terms of strict justice. He said that the Jews could not expect special treatment because of Abraham. Religious communities who lack the energy that love gives, instead of getting involved in the struggle to build a more human community, tend to retreat into a comfort zone for themselves, and look back to an imaginary golden age in the past.

John saw his Baptism as one possible way to escape the judgment that he saw coming. But Baptism on its own would not work without social justice. The religious leaders ignored John. But public sinners, such as tax-collectors and soldiers, were able to respond to the call to repentance when it was rolled-out in simple terms.

John the Baptist was well aware of his missionary limitations. His mission was to prepare the way for Jesus. The Jewish religion had no rites of purification that could wash away the sins of the nation, at this time. The Jewish religion had become legalistic. It had replaced the original vision of justice and love with an endless stream of commands and reprimands, prohibitions and punishments. It had turned the God of Abraham into a sort of cosmic policeman. Legalism is a childish attempt to bargain with God. Keeping commandments is a poor substitute for love. The lover has to give everything, including himself. There is no doubt that the Baptist looked forward to a new age - the age of the Messiah. He said that the Messiah would use a winnowing-fan to separate the wheat from the chaff.

According to St Luke, John said that the Messiah would bring a new kind of Baptism, a Baptism with the Holy Spirit and with fire. It is hard to know what John could have meant at that early stage in sacred history. Every account of the gospel has to reflect something of the self-understanding of the community that the gospel is written for. The gospel writer is, of course, guided by the Holy Spirit.

Discussion Questions

Who are the poor?

Are there any prophetic voices speaking for the poor today?

Why did John say that Baptism, without social justice, would not be enough?

Jewish religion at the time had too many rules and commandments - what was missing?

Why does the church need to promote justice and love?

Are too many rules and commandments a childish attempt to bargain with God?

Can commandments be made into a substitute for love?

Does a disciple have to do more than keep commandments? Does he have to keep Jesus' new commandment of love?

What is different about Jesus' Baptism?

4th Sunday of Advent
Blessed among women
Luke 1: 39-44

Here St Luke tells us that Mary journeyed from the province of Galilee to visit her kinswoman Elizabeth in a town in Judah. In Mary the New Testament goes to visit John and Elizabeth, who represent the Old Testament. The gospel events begin in the context of a great Prophetic inspiration. Inspired by the Spirit and Mary's greeting, Elizabeth is able to herald the significance of what is happening at this moment. As a Prophetess she is able to greet Mary as the mother of her Lord and to tell us that Mary and her child belong to the next stage in God's liberating and saving plan (Peake). The faith of Mary and Elizabeth is contrasted here with the failure of Zechariah (Elizabeth's husband) to believe the Lord's word.

For St Luke, Jesus did come to fulfil, and more than fulfil, the Old Testament's Messianic Promise. "The New Testament fulfils the Old Testament, but it does not draw its meaning from the Biblical past but from the Spirit's life-giving creativity" (La Verdiere). In the bible, revelation gets more personal as the tribal wrappings fade into the past.

Mary inherits the Promise from the Old Testament. But she has to go through a painful personal "quantum leap" of faith, to get personally involved in the next stage of God's decisive plan for the liberation and salvation of the human family.

Faith is a lot more than being able to tick the religious boxes of our tribe or community. Christian faith is here Incarnated in Mary's body. It summons the believer to question our tribal traditions and prejudices. There is personal risk involved.

At Vatican II the Christian community was summoned to take a step forward, to take a risk; to become more human and to become a Pilgrim People with the rest of the human family. Do we have the personal faith needed to implement the decisions of the Council at parish, school and family levels?

Discussion Questions

Is Mary making just a social call on her kinswoman here?

What has the Holy Spirit got to do with this meeting?

What is the role of a Prophet or Prophetess in the Bible?

Any Prophets or Prophetesses about today?

Revelation becomes more personal. What does that mean?

What is a "quantum leap" of faith?

Does faith have to be incarnated in a personal and social way?

Is it easy to implement the decision of Vatican II, at parish and school level?

The Season of Christmas
Peace on Earth

Christmas Night
Peace on Earth
Luke 2: 1-14

"Caesar Augustus issued a decree for a census of the whole world to be taken... while Quirinius was governor of Syria".

We may well wonder why St Luke should go to the trouble of weaving a social and political message into the religious message of the manger. The answer is simple. While Jesus is born in solidarity with the poor and downtrodden, he is also the light of the nations. Jesus is not a celebrity. He is not born to the sound of a media scrum and flash-bulb digital photography. He is more likely born to the sound of sheep and lambs. But he has a family, even if they are homeless on this occasion.

Herod the Great is already plotting the death of the child. The Roman Emperor used to say that is was safer to be Herod's pig than Herod's son, because he had murdered two of his own sons. We can suspect that the shepherds didn't worry too much about Herod as they listened to the angel's anthem. The angels suggest that there is no need to be afraid of Herod. It is not a disaster to be human, provided that we are not under the spell of the works and pomp of Hollywood and provided that we share what we have.

The manger can give us the courage that we need today to say a fond farewell to the grand model of the church that was the Gothic cathedral, with its magnificent stained glass and stonework. This is happening anyway, with more than a few Parish churches having to close down. This is an opportunity to welcome the new grass-roots model of the church that is emerging. This is a simpler, more human and personal model.

The new model challenges us to take the risk of coming closer to each other and to support each other's faith, at a time when the secular culture is beginning to lose its humanity and become a professional mechanical administration.

To be fully itself, to be fully human and Christian, the church has to take on the hopes and dreams of the human family, especially the hopes and dreams of those who can find no room in the Inn.

The magi, the wise men from the east will soon journey to the manger. They too need to hear the Glad tidings of liberation and salvation that Jesus has come to announce.

St Luke does not want us to think of the church as a religious ghetto! The manger is a world-changing event, a liberating and saving event and happening in a backward place, from humble beginnings.

Discussion Questions

Why is St Luke interested in the Roman Empire?

Why was Jesus born in Bethlehem?

Is there something special about the poor?

Why is the Nativity a time to celebrate?

Do we have to welcome a simpler grass-roots model of the church today?

Why was there no room in the Inn for the poor?

Is there much room for the non-Christian in our church today?

Why were the shepherds the first to journey to the manger?

Why was King Herod (and Jerusalem) afraid?

The Holy Family
Why were you looking for me?
Luke 2: 41-52

On this occasion, the Holy Family are on an official visit to the temple on the feast of the Passover. After being lost for three days (he was 12 years old), Jesus reminds his parents that children have to grow up. He asked, "Why were you looking for me? Did you not know that I must be on my Father's business?" St Luke says that his parents did not understand what he said. At this point, Mary didn't say, "I'm tired now and anyway I have to do the washing and then I have to watch Coronation St". St Luke says that she continued to reflect on what Jesus had said.

No matter how strong the family (or community) bond may be, the individuals in the family have personal responsibilities that are wider than the family. Children have, for example, to become adult human beings and adult Christians. The family is crucial when in the modern world the family and the responsibility of becoming human are under pressure.

Mary and Joseph are reminded here that they have to become more than parents. They have to become disciples of Jesus. At times they will struggle to understand what he is saying. The gospel is not as ready-made as we used to think. We have to prepare the way for Jesus to come into our family and into the local community.

Parents today often feel that the children are growing up too fast! In the traditional village, village folk helped the children to grow up. How? By looking out for them and by reminding them of village customs and obligations - even the folktales were a help. It meant that folk had time for each other. At school today, the children sometimes give the impression of being in a zoo, protected by wire fences. We are encouraged to say that it is for the children's protection. The problem is that the local people and parents have no say in the erection of the fences.

Must we prepare today for Jesus to come into our family? To prepare for his coming we have to get used to the idea that the gospel is not ready-made. It is not like the ready-made bread that we buy in the supermarket. It is something that has to be rediscovered, in an original way each day.

Listening to the gospel as an individual is great but more is needed. We need to listen to it as part of a small grass-roots parish community. The gospel does not come alive until it passes through the humanity of the local Christian community. That is when the fat hits the fan.

Discussion Questions

Why were the parents of Jesus upset?

Why did they not understand what Jesus said?

Do parents today find it easy to understand the children?

Are parents today able to learn something from the children?

Do parents today find it easy to let the children grow up?

What are the pressures on the family today?

How can Christian families support each other today?

Do Parents today need the support of a grass roots parish community?

The Epiphany
The Wise Men came from the east bearing gifts
Matthew 2: 1-12

The Wise Men represent the Gentiles. According to Scripture every human being has to come to the manger in one way or another. They do not have to be commanded or threatened with terrible consequences. Coming to Jesus is always a joyful adventure.

This is the way that the Prophet Isaiah sees it: "Arise, shine out, for your light has come. The glory of the Lord is rising on you, though night still covers the earth. The nations come to your light, and kings to your dawning brightness. The riches of the sea will flow to you, the wealth of the nations come to you. Everyone in Sheba will come, bringing gold and incense and singing the praises of the Lord" (60, 1-6).

Part of the way, the Wise Men were guided by a star. St Matthew tells us that the Wise Men did not come empty-handed. They brought gold and other gifts.

Likewise, the human person and the human community never come to Jesus empty-handed. They bring the sacred treasure that the human person is. The human person is the work of his hands. The human community brings the treasures that it already has.

The Second Vatican Council (The Church Today 22) tells us that grace accompanies every human person, and the human community, as they journey towards a meeting with the Christian church and a meeting with Jesus. This journey can be costly, because we all have to get involved in the historical struggle for justice and peace, freedom and love. Without trying to use other people, cheating life, skipping the difficult parts and lying to ourselves and others.

It is by facing the difficult questions about human development that the individual and the community prepare to meet Jesus and his gospel. Human development is a major question for the church today, because it has to rediscover, in a new age, how to dialogue with the human family.

St Matthew tells us that the Wise-Men could not reach the manger without instructions from the People of God (the Jews). "Some Wise-Men came to Jerusalem from the east, 'Where is the infant king of the Jews?' they asked".

All the treasures that the human community bring to Jesus have to be tested in the fiery furnace of the Word of Jesus. The gospel.

Discussion Questions:

Is coming to Jesus a joyful adventure?

"The wealth of the nations will come to you". What does the Prophet mean?

Does grace accompany all human development?

Why did the Wise Men bring gold and gifts?

Is the struggle for justice and love important to Jesus?

Does the church today have to rediscover how to share talents with the human community?

What was the significance of the star?

Why did the Wise Men have to stop at Jerusalem and ask for directions?

Does the wealth of the nations have to be tested in the fiery furnace of the gospel?

The Baptism of the Lord
He will Baptize you with the Holy Spirit
Luke 3: 15-16, 21-22

St Luke gives us a short version of Jesus' Baptism which signals Jesus' solidarity with the downtrodden, one of St Luke's favourite themes. But St Luke does not say (as in Saints Mark and Matthew), that Jesus came from Nazareth to be baptised. And there is no dialogue between Jesus and John. For St Luke, John the Baptist belongs to the past. Don't forget that St Luke is writing for the Gentile church. So St Luke sets out to reinterpret Jesus' Baptism. St Luke is, of course, guided by the Spirit of Jesus.

This ability of the church, guided by the Spirit, to reinterpret the life and mission of Jesus, is of great importance to the church today. Why? Because the church today has to reinterpret the life and mission of Jesus for our secular age. St Luke was writing for a religious age. That is, when religion came naturally, as naturally as the air that we breathe. Of course a lot of religion in Luke's time was pagan religion In any case, St Luke transforms the baptismal event into a descent of the Holy Spirit "The heavens opened and the Spirit of God came down on him". The Spirit is the creative force of Jesus' life and mission (1, 35).

In the Acts of the Apostles (1, 35), also written by St Luke, the descent of the Holy Spirit on the church is also interpreted as a Baptism. Writing in the Acts of the Apostles, St Luke tells us that, on some occasions the Jews contradicted everything that Paul said (2Tim. 4,14). Paul was tested in other ways as well, "Five times from the Jews I received forty lashes minus one. Three times I was beaten with rods. Once I received a stoning. Three times I was shipwrecked; for a night and a day I was adrift at sea. In danger from my own people, in danger from Gentiles" (2Cor. 11, 24).

We'll probably say that this opposition to the gospel that Paul was preaching was terrible. Maybe it was. But maybe this opposition is precisely what keeps the church from going to sleep. That is, living in the past. The modern world is asking serious questions about human development, as it struggles for equality and fraternity.

As Fr Segundo, S.J. says, "Science has the power to transform our image of man". This poses questions for the church. It challenges some of the 19th century image of man and woman. Members of the church and of the human community are expecting the church to face these new questions with faith in reason and in the guidance of the Holy Spirit, and to be able to face these questions boldly and in a creative way. That was what St Luke was doing in his time.

The church cannot use a 19th century image of man (his hopes and dreams) to preach the gospel today. The children will tell us how we are doing!

Discussion Questions:

St Luke was writing for Gentiles. Is that why he talks about Baptism in the Holy Spirit?

Does dialogue with the human community (or opposition) help the church?

Does the church need dialogue with the human community today?

How do the questions that are asked in today's secular culture, help the church?

Does the modern world ask new questions about becoming human?

Can the church speak boldly today, like St Paul?

Can the church depend on the guidance of the Holy Spirit today?

Does the Holy Spirit empower the church to overcome the obstacles that stand in the way of the gospel today?

Can a person become a Christian without becoming human?

The Season of Lent

1st Sunday in Lent
Jesus is tempted in the wilderness
Luke 4: 1-13

The Jews spent 40 years in the wilderness. The wilderness has no ready-made roads, or comfort zones that human individuals or communities can escape into. Here individuals and communities are tested. They discover, or fail to discover, what it means to be human. They also discover the temptation to evade responsibility for human and Christian development. Religious people are prone to use religion to protect themselves from the call to take their own and others human development seriously.

This is what happens here with Jesus. The devil invites him (when he is hungry and vulnerable) to bypass his humanity and to use his divine power. Jesus cannot do that because he is on a mission to liberate and save the whole human family. A humanity that has to be liberated and saved in a human way.

Beginning with Jesus, the human family has to be empowered to play a creative and responsible role in its own liberation and salvation. Jesus has to involve himself, in a fully human way in the historical human drama, in the struggle to overcome hunger and disease and to promote justice, freedom and human rights. When the struggle becomes difficult, the temptation to cut corners, to cut and run, can become fierce. God is the first port of call for the religious person who wants to escape. We want God to take over our creative responsibilities! When that fails, we try to get the poor to become our servants and slaves. Religious communities are tempted to do the same thing. In the old days, and the not so old (!), the church was tempted to think of humanity as its servant, despite what the gospel says.

In the temptations of Jesus, St Luke reminds us of another temptation that can be a bottomless pit for self-deception. It has to do with power. Here the individual and the community are tempted to elbow their way into positions of power. St Luke says that, "for a small consideration", as they say (!), the devil promises Jesus unlimited political power! In the West, injustice and the abuse of power is still not taken seriously. In the Western world today, the only sins that are taken seriously are sins that have to do with sexuality! We have to suspect that the people in power have a vested interest in promoting that line.

Vatican II told us that we should forget the idea that the Christian community is totally independent of the human community. That we should forget the idea that the church has all the answers; that the human and Christian communities need ready-made answers wrapped in plastic! That was a system that worked very well in the middle ages, but is not tolerable today.

Vatican II said that the church is, "A leaven and a kind of soul for human society" (The Church Today, 40). But that does not mean that the leaven and the soul are ready made, and pre-prepared without reference to human society.

Vatican II goes on to say that, "The church is joined with the rest of men in the search for truth" (The Church Today, 16) It goes on, "The church labours to discern the signs of God's presence and purpose in the happenings, needs and desires in which this People (i.e. the People of God) has a part along with other men of our age" (The Church Today, 11).

Discussion Questions

Is the desert a place of self-discovery?

What is going on in Jesus' first temptation?

Does Jesus have to take responsibility for human liberation and salvation?

Empowered by Jesus, does the human family have to take creative responsibility for its own development?

What are hungry people tempted to do today?

What is wrong with focussing on the salvation of our individual souls?

How is religion (or God) used as an escape from human responsibility?

Does the church have all the answers? Can it just tell the human community what to do and what not to do?

Can the human community help the Christian community to search for the truth?

Can the Christian Laity and the Priest help each other to explore the Scriptures?

Is it easy for Christians to avoid elbowing their way into positions of power in the church?

Does power corrupt today?

2nd Sunday of Lent
As Jesus prayed, the aspect of his face changed
Luke 9: 28-36

This is a mysterious part of the gospel. To see the direction that we are going here, we might think of the words of Jesus, "I have given them the glory that you gave to me".

St Luke helps us to expand on St Mark's account of the Transfiguration. He says that on the holy mountain Moses and Elijah were talking with Jesus about his Exodus that would happen shortly in Jerusalem (9, 31). In the first Exodus, Moses led the Israelites from slavery in Egypt to freedom in the Promised Land. It involved a perilous journey through the deep, through the sea. Now Jesus has to lead the whole human race from a deeper slavery (sin), to a more personal freedom.

St Luke says that it was while he was praying that Jesus was transfigured. He also says that, "A cloud covered them with shadow". In St Matthew's account of the same event, we are told that it was "A bright cloud". Strangely enough, at this point, St Luke seems to be focussing on Jesus' humanity. When Jesus has to pass through the darkness of the cross, it is humanity that is vulnerable. This helps to explain why he has to pray for the strength of the Holy Spirit, "the power of the most High". Here the "Bright cloud" stands for the Holy Spirit. And then the Father's voice is heard. To reassure the disciple that Jesus, despite his human condition, is the Son and servant of God.

We need to remind ourselves that in the Bible liberating and saving events are foreshadowed, to give us time to prepare for the mystical event itself. Here the Transfiguration foreshadows the resurrection. The Transfiguration comes six days after Jesus told the disciples the shocking news that he was to be a suffering Messiah. We need to get used to the idea that somehow we do not begin to understand the Transfiguration, until we begin to make it happen, in some small way at least, for other people.

When Jesus says, "The glory that you gave to me, I have given to them", he is not talking about the dim and distant future. Biblically speaking, the glory in question here is being foreshadowed now. And we have a creative part in making it happen.

How? We can presume that the disciples, who were present on this occasion, played some part in Jesus' Transfiguration. We too can help our families and communities to experience something of Jesus' Transfiguration, by being there for them in times of joy and sorrow. Without this experience, how could we enter into the mystery of Jesus' transfiguration?

Discussion Questions

What was Jesus' Exodus?

Jesus had to lead us to a deeper personal freedom?

What has prayer got to do with this event?

What is the "bright cloud"?

Was Jesus vulnerable at this point?

Is this event related to the cross?

How does the transfiguration foreshadow the resurrection?

Do we have to experience the transfiguration here and now?

Do we have a creative part in helping others to experience something of the transfiguration?

3rd Sunday of Lent
Unless you repent they will all perish as they did
Luke 13: 1-9

Originally this gospel had to do with the Jewish nation. And especially with the Jewish religious leaders, who refused to accept Jesus and his gospel. In the parable of the fig-tree, Jesus says that they have one last chance.

But St Luke is not a Jew. He is a Christian. He is mainly interested in what is happening, and failing to happen, within the Christian and human communities in his time. As the Christian community gets more involved in the pagan world, its leaders are tempted to confuse positions of importance, in the church and society, with holiness. St Luke is saying that Christian leaders are not sufficiently critical of themselves and of pagan society. The danger here is that what we call the laity will not be given creative responsibility for the development of the community. When that happens, the community will be ill-prepared to respond to the challenges of the pagan world.

The fig-tree here is a disappointment, not because it is bearing poisonous fruit and toxic chemicals, but because it is not bearing good fruit. All it is bearing is poor quality timber.

Here Jesus is promoting a more personal understanding of sin. "He is saying that there is no connection between sin and the misfortunes that happen to us, whether they come in human form (Pilate 13, 1), or whether their cause is accidental (v.4)" (Gutierrez).

In the old days, we had difficulty in escaping from the idea that poverty, disease and misfortune are due to our own sins. Jesus says that they are not. Once we start to worry about ourselves and our individual sin, real or imaginary, we can easily go on to think of God as a cosmic policeman who suffers from legalism and has a plot to punish us! The serious point is that once we get hooked on ourselves, we'll find it had to witness to Jesus in the wider world.

Why is that? Worrying about ourselves burns too much of our emotional energy. It also robs us of the confidence that we need to feed the hungry and set the downtrodden free. This is especially relevant to the church today, when the church is trying to, as it were, to plant new fig trees. The church today is trying to find a new model for its life and mission. It has to rediscover how to evangelise our secular age.

Vatican II tells us that the church does not have ready made answers to every question that arises (The Church Today, 16). The Christian laity, who are nearest to the coal-face of the modern world, need to have a more active and responsible part to play in making the life and mission of Jesus their own. And having a creative part in interpreting the gospel for the church and the human community.

Discussion Questions

Why was the Jewish religious establishment not bearing fruit?

Is the Christian church ever in danger of not bearing fruit?

What fruit is in question here?

How could failing to do something be so bad? (The fig tree was not bearing toxic or poisonous fruit).

Do we spend too much time worrying about ourselves and our sins? And not enough time witnessing to Jesus in the human community?

Is there a connection between sin and the misfortunes that we meet?

Do we need the personal support of each other as we try to live the gospel in the modern secular world?

Are Christians too individualistic today?

Is the faith of isolated Christians vulnerable to attack today?

Do we need grass-roots Parish communities today?

4th Sunday of Lent
Your brother here was dead and has come back to life
Luke 15: 1-3, 11-32

This is one of our favourite parables, but that does not mean that we know that we understand it that well. Here St Luke invites us to see the difference between pre-Christian (Rabbinic-Jewish) and Christian morality. St Luke is writing for a Christian community that is tempted to go back to a pre-Christian model of morality.

The two sons in question here are typical disciples of Jesus at the time. They both put their father to the test. They are both thinking of God as a sort of Jewish cosmic policeman, who puts the fear of God into everybody. The elder son thinks of himself as a slave, "I have slaved for you, and never disobeyed your commandments". And when the younger son returns, he asks his father to, "Make me as one of your paid servants".

We are entitled to think that the younger son may have been bored by the endless cycle of rules and commandments (rules and commandments that are not supported by love are, according to St Paul, "A burden too heavy to bear"). The younger son wanders away from home to get a bit of freedom and feel more human. But his adventures went badly wrong and he ended up living with the pigs, in a pagan land.

Both sons are invited to rediscover the Christian God who has one new commandment, to love unconditionally. When the prodigal son comes home, he does not expect to be treated as a son, "Treat me as one of your paid servants". What actually happens is that his father anticipates his return. His father sees him coming, "From a long way off". His father shows no interest in a trial, a court-marshal or legalism. The important thing is that the prodigal son is home, as a son. He was dead and has come back to life. It is time to kill the fatted calf and make merry. The Christian God forgives unconditionally. Forgiveness is new life. A new creation, as St. Paul says.

The biggest danger for a disciple of Jesus today is that he will have difficulty in believing in unconditional forgiveness. In our capitalist culture, we are inclined to believe that everything has to be earned, or bought at a price. The problem with Christian forgiveness is that it cannot be earned, and to begin to understand it, we have to forgive the people who offend us and offend the community. If we try to earn forgiveness, the danger is that we'll start worrying about ourselves. We will waste any amount of emotional energy, and have little left for evangelising the modern world – which is our Christian mission.

In the parable, the father does not take sides. He wants both sons at home in a family that loves and forgives unconditionally.

Discussion Questions

Is this your favourite parable?

Why did the younger son wander away from home?

What is a cosmic policeman?

Was the Christian community under the spell of a Jewish-type morality at the time?

Why did the elder son say that he had slaved for his father?

Did the elder son have attitude?

Why did the father not punish the prodigal son?

Is Christian forgiveness unconditional? And if so, why?

Why did the father kill the fatted calf?

Do we find it easy to forgive today?

Do we find it easy to accept forgiveness today?

Can forgiveness be earned?

5th Sunday of Lent
"Woman where are they?"
John 8: 1-11

There is a lot of sin involved here but most of it is hidden. Every big community (political or religious), need a big institution to manage it, but as time goes on, the mission statement of the institution (i.e. what it exists to do) can get sidelined. Then the community is tempted to become rigid, mechanical and focussed on itself – to secure itself against the changes that time tends to bring. Now the community is in danger of losing some of its humanity. And it may begin to look like a military force.

Here in this episode, the top-brass of the religious institution is trying to trap Jesus on the horns of a dilemma. And they are using the adulteress as bait. A woman involved in adultery could be stoned to death. A man's adultery was much less serious! And don't forget that it was men who made the law in the first place! If Jesus says that she should not be stoned, they will accuse him of not keeping the Law.

St Luke says that they made the woman stand there in front of everyone. A poor woman, who was probably exploited by men in the first place. Now she is stared at, humiliated, afraid, devalued, rejected by the community, clinging to what is left of her humanity.

Meanwhile, Jesus is writing on the ground, or diverting his eyes to spare her further embarrassment. But Jesus' focus is on the future. To turn the situation around, Jesus asks a question. He asks the woman a question! In the sound of his voice she knows that the worst is over. He has established a personal link with her. His mission is to set the downtrodden free. And she can help him, in a small way, to make public his gospel of mercy and love.

As the church draws closer to the human community today, as it must do (see Vatican II, The Church Today, 16) there is a danger that the church's life and mission could become more scientific, mechanical and professional.

This temptation can be avoided in the same way as Jesus does here. We have to suspect that he was sitting on the ground. The church can enter into dialogue with the Christian Laity and the wider human community, provided that it can identify with the community in a human and personal way. "You have hidden these things from the learned and clever, and revealed them to mere children".

Discussion Questions

Why do institutions tend to become mechanical?

Why did the religious establishment turn on this poor woman?

Has the religious establishment lost something and more than something of its humanity here?

Why did Jesus write on the ground?

Are we surprised that Jesus spoke to the woman?

Does Jesus always focus on the future?

Does the church have to build any bridges with the human community today?

Why did the religious establishment here care so little about this woman?

Why was the religious establishment using this woman as bait?

Passion Sunday
I have longed to eat this Passover with you
Luke 22: 14-23, 56

In scripture, Holy Thursday, Good Friday and Easter Sunday are one event. If we separate the cross and resurrection, as we in the west tend to do, then the cross and resurrection begin to lose their mystery and their Biblical meaning. Once they are separated, the resurrection tends to become just another miracle, instead of what it really is - the dawn of a new age for the human family.

Our western interpretations of the gospel tend to be Biblically weak, because our culture is too individualistic. Not sufficiently focussed on the community.

St Luke starts off here by telling us (22, 2), that Jesus longed to eat the Passover with his disciples. The original Passover had to do with the liberation of the Jewish people from slavery in Egypt, to freedom in the Promised Land. Now Jesus' Passover (by the cross and resurrection) will lead the whole human community to a deeper freedom from slavery, to the freedom in the kingdom of justice and love that Jesus is establishing.

St Luke wants us to understand that the cross is a mystery that cannot be fully explained by the opposition of the Jewish leaders to Jesus. He says that Satan is in action here. Satan represents a mysterious darkness that we get glimpses of today, in the drugs industry, the gambling industry (even the banks are involved!), the war industry and so on.

The Passover was not to be the Passover of Jesus alone, but of Jesus with his disciples. "Go and prepare the Passover for us, that we may eat it" (22, 8).

Jesus' sacrifice here is a personal one, rather than an impersonal pagan one. Jesus dies and rises again with anybody who is poor or oppressed. Without his solidarity with the poor, it would be hard to express the cross in a human and personal way.

To bring this point out, St Luke tells us that Jesus celebrated the Eucharist at the heart of the Passover drama. The Eucharist is celebrated in the form of a meal. The Eucharist looks back to the mystery of the cross and resurrection, but it also looks forward to a new age when everybody will have bread on the table, because bread means life when we have it. It is, for example, at the family meal that the family comes back to life. At the family meal, past misunderstandings are forgiven and forgotten. And the members of the family renew their commitment to the family bond of love.

Discussion Questions:

Is the passion of Jesus more than a drama of Jesus on his own?

Does the resurrection help us to understand the cross?

Is there a difference between a Christian and a pagan sacrifice?

How does the cross of Jesus help us today?

How does the resurrection help us today?

Are there any signs of the resurrection in Britain or Ireland today?

How does Jesus' solidarity with the poor help us to understand the cross?

Why did Jesus long to eat the Passover with his disciples?

What was the Passover?

St Luke says that Satan is active here. What does that mean?

Why did Jesus celebrate the Eucharist at the heart of the Passover?

The Season of Easter

Easter Vigil
Look for Jesus among the living
Luke 24: 1-12

The first thing that the gospel has to witness to here is that the tomb was empty. It would be pointless to say that Jesus is risen, without saying that he is risen in his human body, because his human body is the body that he suffered in – in his solidarity with the poor and downtrodden and in his solidarity with the whole human family - as the new Adam.

Rising again in his human body (which the disciples have to witness to) is a celebration, a victory over the dark, Satanic and sinful forces of injustice that devalue the human community. And deprive it of life. In rising again, Jesus rises again in solidarity with any human person who has been devalued, humiliated and deprived of a life that is more human here and now. Jesus' resurrection is a victory of life and love over the concrete, historical forces of death.

Two thirds of the human community today suffer from hunger and malnutrition. Up to 30 million of them die every year from hunger and malnutrition. Christians living in the rich countries have to take responsibility for what happens in the 3rd world, as they call it. Worrying about ourselves, and the number of Parishes that are closing in our Diocese, will not get us very far - we need to start thinking outside the traditional box.

Some Christians still have the childish tendency to see the resurrection as just another miracle! They also have difficulty in explaining how the resurrection relates to the cross.

A disciple of Jesus has to do more than listen to sermons on the resurrection of Jesus. He or she has to have some personal experience of what the resurrection of Jesus means to us now. Somehow we have to meet Jesus himself. And we can meet him especially in the poor and downtrodden. That is what St Matthew says (25, 30).

What I'm saying here is that we have to get involved in the

struggles to liberate the human individual and the human community from the forces that oppress them. What we fail to do for those in need may be the very thing that keeps us from experiencing the resurrection of Jesus in a personal way. It is difficult to understand the mystery of the resurrection until we see some oppressed person being freed from his or her chains. And it works better if we help to do it! It is when we see people coming back to life (in some way), that we know that Jesus is risen.

Discussion Questions

Is the resurrection more than another miracle?

Should we look for Jesus among the living?

Why are we told that the tomb was empty? How does that help us today?

Is the resurrection related, in some way, to the cross?

If BBC television was there on Easter Sunday morning, would it help us now?

How can we experience the resurrection of Jesus, in a personal way now, like the Apostles?

How can the resurrection of Jesus help the millions of people who die of hunger every year, in the 3rd world?

2nd Sunday of Easter
The Doubting Thomas
John 20: 19-31

St Thomas is a modern sort of man! He refuses to believe without some kind of proof! It is the wounds in his hands and side that identifies Jesus for Thomas. In effect, Jesus now tells the Apostles and us that the church's priority is not contemplative prayer. The church's priority is to open the church to the world, and witness to the resurrection of Jesus and to his life and mission.

The faith of the church has to be translated into works that give life. "The spirit (of Jesus) will be with the church, so that it can speak about God and man, but only in terms of Jesus' life, death and resurrection" (Gutierrez).

The disciples have to forgive sin. Sin is more than an offence against God. It is also an offence against men and women. Sin is destructive of life. It involves all sorts of attempts to deceive people. To oppress, enslave, devalue and crucify them – the cross reminds us in a shocking way.

The biggest temptation today will be the temptation to bypass the humanity of Jesus, and go straight to his Divinity. The doubting Thomas reminds us what we have to do. As I was saying, it is the wounds in the hands and side of Jesus that activates Thomas' belief. The question then arises for us - can we see anything of the wounds of Jesus today? Guided by St Matthew's gospel, we are entitled to believe that the wounds of Jesus become visible again for us in the faces and lives of the poor and downtrodden "As long as you did it to the least of these, you did it to me" (Matthew 25, 30).

To see these wounds we need to see them close up. We need to do more than this. Helping the downtrodden is a way of giving life and bringing life out of the death that the poor suffer (30 million die of malnutrition annually), gives a first hand experience of the resurrection of Jesus.

When Jesus came to the Apostles on Easter Sunday, the doors were closed. Once the Passover was over, the disciples were afraid of what the Jews might do. The disciples would then be tempted to become defensive, rather than risk their lives in witnessing to Jesus in a hostile city and culture.

The temptation persists today. The church is tempted to perpetuate an older model of the church, rather than translating it, with the help of Vatican II, into a language that the modern world can understand.

It can be done. The Catholic church in Latin America (which has nearly half the membership of the Catholic Church world wide), has gone a long way towards translating the gospel into a language that the modern secular world can understand.

Discussion Questions

Why does the doubting Thomas want to see the wounds of Jesus?

Where can we see the wounds of Jesus today?

Why must the church be open to the world?

The faith of the church has to be translated into works that give life here and now. What does that mean?

The Spirit will help the church to speak of God and man, but only in terms of the life, death and resurrection of Jesus. What does that mean today?

Is sin more than an offence against God?

How does helping the downtrodden give us a more personal understanding of the life and mission of Jesus?

Why were the doors closed when Jesus came?

Are there any doors of the church or the human community closed today?

3rd Sunday of Easter
Simon, son of John, do you love me?
John 21: 1-19

The apostle John has already told us that Jesus appeared to Mary Magdalen, and to the disciples behind closed doors. Now he appears to the disciples as they resume their daily work of fishing. Once Jesus has risen in his humanity, his mission is universal. His mission has to do with giving life. With communicating his risen life to the whole human community. His presence indicates that life overcomes death for those who believe in Jesus' life-giving work.

Jesus again celebrates a meal with his disciples. Food gives life and fellowship. All of Jesus' meals herald and foreshadow a new age when everybody will have food on the table. In our time, millions of people still die of malnutrition every year. Here Jesus is preparing and empowering his community to witness to his liberating and saving work in a hostile world.

Peter is repeatedly asked to affirm that he loves Jesus. At its deepest level, the church is a mystery of love. Don't forget that the writer of this gospel is, "The disciple that Jesus loved". But the church also has an institutional aspect, which is another gift of the Spirit. This is where St Peter comes in. In a moment of weakness he denied the Lord on three occasions on Good Friday. He failed to risk his life for Jesus in a moment of danger. Here his authority is being restored.

The point is that the office holder in the church is like a lamb among wolves. He will often be tempted not to risk his life for his sheep. To flee when he sees the wolf coming! In our time he will be tempted to cling to an outdated model of the church's ministry, because it is easier. It is easier for him, but harder for the children who want to believe in Jesus.

St John, the beloved Disciple, appears to be telling us that, at its deepest level, the church is a mystery of love. And that Peter's charism (i.e. gift of the Spirit), needs to be balanced with the gift of the Spirit of love that John represents. St John's charism has to do with a more personal approach to the gospel. But all gifts of the Spirit are complementary.

Both Apostles have to "follow" Jesus. After this he said, "Follow me". St John says that after the other disciples had fled, the beloved Disciple remained near Jesus' cross (19, 26), and witnessed his death (19, 34). Later, when the beloved Disciple and Peter went to the tomb, and found the body gone, the beloved Disciple believed on the spot that Jesus was risen (20, 8), while Peter needed an appearance of Jesus before he believed. In the final chapter of the gospel, Peter could not recognise Jesus standing on the shore of the Sea of Galilee, without the assistance of the beloved Disciple (21,7) (Raymond E. Brown, John the Evangelist).

Discussion Questions:

Why did Jesus appear to the disciples while they were fishing?

Do we meet Jesus while we are working today?

Why did Jesus eat a meal on this occasion?

Why do people die of malnutrition today?

Why did Jesus ask Peter about love for himself?

How does the ministry of Peter differ from St John's?

Does Peter's denial of Jesus on Good Friday carry a message for the church today?

How close is the church to the human family?

4th Sunday of Easter
The sheep that belong to me listen to my voice?
John 10: 27-30

Here Jesus continues to tell us about the Good Shepherd and his flock. He says that the sheep that belong to him listen to his voice. Or listen to his Word. There is more involved in listening to the Word of Jesus than just reading the Scriptures. To begin with, the word of Jesus does not become fully alive for us until it passed through the humanity of the local Christian community. Until the local Christian community makes the Word their own, when they take it into the heart of the human community where they live and work today.

And then the Word of Jesus has to get past the ambushes that the disciples meet. One leading Latin American theologian (Fr. Comblin) says that one of the worst ambushes can come from the experts who set out with the best intentions to protect the Word! What do they do? "They so institutionalise, ritualise and formalise God's Word that, though recited daily, it loses all meaning, all resonance in the world. The other way is to overlook - discreetly - the evil done by the powerful, so as to avoid persecution. Obviously, the church has never officially abandoned God's Word. It celebrates it in worship, proclaims it in its preaching, teaches it in its schools. But the Word can be celebrated in a way that is equivalent to silence. Proclaimed without reference or application to concrete realities".

Another popular way to distort the Word of Jesus has to do with bypassing Jesus' humanity, and focussing on his divinity. When we focus on Jesus' humanity, as he walks the dusty roads of Galilee, we begin to feel guilty when we fail to focus on our social responsibilities. For example, when we fail to help the poor person who has "fallen among robbers" we begin to feel guilty.

The quickest way to bypass the small print of Jesus' Word is to think of Jesus as simply God. Then we can goof off on a phoney spiritual journey that has less inconvenient roots in the human or Christian communities!

Discussion Questions

Does reading the Bible bring us close enough to Jesus today?

Is there such a thing as a false peace?

Why does Jesus attack a false peace?

Any traces of a false peace about today?

Should we just follow the community and not ask critical questions?

Does a disciple have to take some responsibility for human and Christian development?

Does the Christian community have to compete with the secular world today?

Does the community have to promote justice as well as peace?

How does Jesus help us to promote justice and peace?

What kinds of people are opposed to Jesus and his gospel?

5th Sunday of Easter
I give you a new commandment. Love one another
John 13: 31-35

Jesus has to depart soon, but he will continue to be among the disciples if they continue to live according to his new commandment. "A new commandment I give you, that you love one another, as I have loved you".

Some people may think that Jesus' new commandment should simply be added to the commandments that we already have. Most of them from the Old Testament. No.

Jesus' mission has to do with revealing, for the first time, a mystery kept hidden for generations, as St Paul says. The mystery is God's unlimited love for humanity, made visible, human and historical in Jesus Christ.

This means that Jesus has to reinterpret all the Scriptures, traditions and commandments that were there already. This means that all the old commandments have to be reinterpreted in the light of his new commandment.

And how did Jesus love us? Jesus' priority was not to preserve his life and reputation with walls and gates and golden temples.

Jesus' mission had to do with being a servant, risking his life to liberate and save the human family. And he sends the church to do the same.

This new commandment is something that the church has to learn every day, by listening to the word of Jesus, and to the questions and problems that arise within the human community.

Why should the church listen to the human community today?

Well, in recent times, the human community has been very active in asking questions about human rights, justice and peace, equality, freedom and so on. Vatican II tells us that the church's dialogue with the human community is not optional.

"Christians are joined with the rest of men in the search for truth, and for the genuine solution to the numerous problems that arise in the life of individuals and from social relationships" (The Church Today, 16).

Listening to the word of Jesus is more complicated that it used to be when we all lived in villages. Life is more complicated in the modern secular city. This means that the word of Jesus has to pass through the local Christian community. Here every member of the community has to play an active and creative part in interpreting the gospel for the local community. The Priest on his own does not have all the gifts of the Spirit.

Discussion Questions

Is Jesus' new commandment just added to the ones we already had?

Does Jesus reinterpret the Scriptures and Old Testament commandments in the light of his new commandment?

What is Jesus' new commandment?

Did Jesus protect himself with gates and walls and alarms?

How does the church protect itself today?

Does the new commandment have to be learned every day?

Are there any special difficulties about listening to the word of Jesus today?

Does the church have to listen to the human community today?

What are gifts of the Spirit?

6th Sunday of Easter
The Holy Spirit will remind you of all that I have said to you.
John 14: 23-29

Here Jesus reassures that while he is leaving them from a physical viewpoint, he will return in a new form. He and the Father will send the Holy Spirit, but that does not mean that Jesus will be replaced by the Holy Spirit! The Holy Spirit does not become incarnate. And the church continues to be the body of Christ. The Spirit will unfold the meaning of the word of Jesus and of Jesus himself for the human community. The Spirit helps the Apostles to begin to understand the life and mission of Jesus and how to take the mystery of Jesus to the Partians, the Medes, the French, and the British (see the Acts of the Apostles).

Without the Holy Spirit the church would be afraid to go beyond its security zone, or its own walls, to claim the world for Christ. The church has to go beyond its comfort zone to promote justice and peace, freedom and human rights. To test everything that is happening, or failing to happen, in the human community, in the light of the gospel.

To do this, the church has to be (as St Paul says) clothed from head to foot in the armour of Christ. In Scripture the Word of Jesus is the sword of the Spirit. The church needs that armour because it has to lay siege to the strongholds that promote injustice and deny basic human rights in a small, or on an industrial scale.

This is where the church has to "Stay awake"! The people, who promote injustice, are not going to tell us that injustice is their speciality! They may not even be aware that they are promoting injustice. Consequently, they have to be smoked out. And then they can turn on us.

Once the church goes into the modern city, it knows that it does not have all the answers, ready-made and pre-packaged, even before the questions are asked! Vatican II tells us that, "Christians are joined with the rest of men in the search for truth, and for the genuine solution to the numerous problems that arise in the life of individuals and from social relationships" (The Church Today, 16).

Jesus now says that he will give the church his own peace - a peace that the world cannot give. There are two kinds of peace. There is the phoney peace that is built on the shifting sands of inequality, injustice, half-truths, dodgy-dossiers and just plain lies. This kind of peace is often supplied by the bully, the caveman, the shepherd who fails to risk his life for his sheep, when he sees the wolf coming.

The peace that Jesus is talking about is built on justice, freedom and human rights. Religious people sometimes think that if they love God, human rights will take care of themselves, or that human rights are not that important. This is a mistake. A disciple of Jesus cannot bypass the Incarnation. If we bypass what is human, how will we get close to the humanity of Jesus?

Discussion Questions

The Holy Spirit unfolds the meaning of Jesus for humanity. What does that mean?

Does the Holy Spirit replace Jesus?

Does the Holy Spirit bring us close to Jesus in a personal way?

Is injustice an obstacle to Jesus' mission?

Does the church have to risk going outside its own walls?

What is a phoney peace? Where might we find one today?

What kind of peace is Jesus talking about?

Does the church have ready-made answers to all the world's questions?

Can the church manage to find the answers without help from the human community?

The Ascension
As he blessed them he was carried up to heaven.
Luke 24: 46-53

St Matthew says nothing about the Ascension. St Matthew and St Mark conclude their gospels with the sending on a mission to preach about the risen Christ. In the light of Easter, they can see the works and words of Jesus in a new light, a new perception. His resurrection was a victory of life over death (Luke 24, 46). Meanwhile, St Luke insists on the physical absence of Jesus. But that does not mean that, once Jesus has ascended, the disciples can stand there looking into the sky. "Men of Galilee, why do you stand there looking into the sky?" (Acts 1,11). Don't forget that it was St Luke who wrote the Acts of the Apostles.

At this point there is no need to panic! The physical absence of Jesus challenges the community to take more adult responsibility for the mission of Jesus and the church. The community has to do more than tick religious boxes as regards the life and mission of Jesus. Guided by the Spirit of Jesus, the church has a creative and personal role. It has to learn how to speak the language of justice and love to the Partians, the Medes, the Europeans and further a field.

The community has to do more than just report what Jesus said and did. The community has to make the life and mission of Jesus its own life and mission. It has to be brave enough to enjoy the freedom from the Law that Jesus enjoyed. It has to have the freedom to love. Otherwise it would not have the courage and stamina that it needs to take on the oppressive forces that stalk the human community. But the community must not attempt to take over from Jesus and the Holy Spirit!

Jesus is more present to the church now than he was when he was physically present. The church can make him visible, because it is his body. But the church is not identical with Jesus. It is his servant! It is his bride as well as his body. The church can make Jesus more and more visible. But that is not automatic. It has to be earned, by surrendering its no-go areas to him, and the Holy Spirit.

Discussion Questions

Were the disciples more prepared for the Ascension after Easter?

What is important about the physical absence of Jesus after his Ascension?

Why do the disciples "Stand there looking into the sky after the Ascension?

Does the community take more responsibility for the mission of Jesus after he has Ascended?

Does the church have to do more than just tick religious boxes after the Ascension? Or does it have a more personal and creative role?

And the hardest question! How does Jesus become visible after his ascension?

Does the church have to have the freedom from the Law that Jesus enjoyed?

Does the church have to have freedom to love?

Does the church ever "Stand there looking into the sky" today?

Pentecost Sunday
Receive the Holy Spirit. As the Father sent me,
I'm sending you.
John 20: 19-23

In St John's gospel, it is still Easter day. The life and mission of the Holy Spirit gets distorted, when detached from Jesus, because the Spirit speaks only in terms of the life, death and resurrection of Jesus.

The first thing that Jesus does here, after his resurrection, is to establish his human identity! He shows them his hands and his side. Once the disciples have received the Holy Spirit, they will be able to recognise Jesus' new humanity, as well as his divinity.

What is different about Jesus' new humanity? It is a humanity that can and must be shared in order to create a new community. Left to ourselves, our humanity is a closed shop. A prey to fear and pathological insecurity - the disciples were lurking behind closed doors, for fear of the Jews. And probably fear of each other as well!

Fear and insecurity tends to rob us of the energy that we need to play a creative part, with Jesus and the Holy Spirit, in the modern struggle for justice and human rights.

The Spirit gives the Apostles the capacity to go beyond being professionals who have only a limited, nine to five, involvement in the life and mission of Jesus. They have to risk life and limb in a life and death struggle with the forces of death (injustice, lack of freedom and human rights, military adventures, are the forces of death) that prowl the modern city. There are forces that promote life at work in the modern city too.

Pentecost is a social as well as a personal event. The Acts of the Apostle talks about a "violent wind" (2, 2). This is a tempest that overthrows the old established order that kept individuals isolated from each other, and unable to speak and practice the mystery of love.

Now the Christian and human community can speak the one language of justice, equality, freedom, human rights and love.

The church today is still trying to rediscover some aspects of the mission of the Holy Spirit. Raymond E. Brown does not seem to get it right when he says, "The likeness of the Spirit to Jesus, enables the Spirit to substitute for him" (John the Evangelist, 92)

The Spirit has major role in the continuing mission of Jesus, but it is the body of Christ (the church) that makes Christ visible. And especially his humanity! If we ever lose sight of Jesus' humanity, we have no fixed anchor. We are vulnerable to dealing with fairy tales. One of the great Father's of the church (Tertullion) used to say, "The flesh is the hinge of salvation".

Discussion Questions

Why does St John say that the Holy Spirit came on Easter Sunday?

Why were the disciples lurking behind closed doors?

Are Christians afraid to witness to Jesus today?

Why did Jesus show them his hands and side?

Does the Spirit help the church to speak in a language that the Partians and Medes can understand?

Do Christians have a private life that is not involved in the mission of Jesus?

Why does the Acts of the Apostles say that there was a violent wind on Pentecost Sunday?

What is different about the new humanity of Jesus?

Can the Holy Spirit substitute for Jesus?

Trinity Sunday
All that the Father has is mine.
John 16: 12-15

Recently, Pope Benedict reminded us that when we go into a city today, we don't see any shrines or monuments to the pagan gods that St Paul had to deal with in his time. So what happened to the pagan gods? The short answer is that the Christian God became man: "All that the Father has is mine".

The Christian God no longer dwells in shrines and temples made by human hands. He has relocated! He comes to us in a human way.

Do we find it easy to relate to Jesus in a human way? No. we all carry some of the genes of the doubting Apostle Thomas. Thomas said to Jesus, "Show us the Father and we'll be satisfied". Jesus replied, "Thomas, I've been with you all this time, and you still don't know me. He who sees me sees the Father". Thomas was looking for a more direct way to God. There are glaring examples of this today, in the Catholic papers and books! They tend to go straight to Jesus' divinity, as if going to his humanity was waste of time! This helps to explain way we have difficulty today in getting the children to believe in Jesus.

It is not possible to believe in Jesus' divinity without first believing in his humanity – which includes his historical mission. Belief in Jesus includes belief in his Gospel and in his historical work to open the eyes of the blind, setting the downtrodden free, and announcing Glad Tidings to the poor.

According to the leading Latin American theologian (Fr Segundo), after his resurrection, Jesus only appeared to people who believe in him when he walked the dusty roads of Israel.

This means that we get close to Jesus (and God) when we liberate our slaves, and get involved in Jesus' historical struggle to live for others, in order to promote justice and peace, freedom and human rights.

Jesus gives us his Spirit (the Spirit of his humanity and divinity), to give us the courage to go beyond our comfort zones. We need to get used to the idea that the sacred that used to be located in shrines and temples made by human hands, has relocated. St Paul says to the Christian community at Corinth that they are the temple of God. We are now at a new stage where we are beginning to see that every human person is a very real and sacred temple of Jesus and God. The same goes for the human community.

St Augustine: "I erred in seeking you outside, when you were within".

Discussion Questions

Why have all the shrines to the pagan gods gone from cities?

Why did the Christian God become man?

Do we find it easy to believe in Jesus' humanity –which includes believing in his historical life and mission?

Like the Apostle, Thomas, do we prefer to go straight to God?

Why do we have to believe in Jesus' humanity, before we can believe in his divinity?

Do we have to believe in Jesus' liberating and saving work, before we can believe in his humanity or divinity?

Is the human person a sacred temple of Jesus and of God today?

Are the Christian and human communities temples of Jesus and of God?

Is this relocation of the sacred important for teaching children today?

Corpus Christi
They all ate as much as they wanted
Luke 9: 11-17

All the four Gospels have the feeding of the 5,000 men. St Matthew includes women and children! St Luke says that the first thing that Jesus does here was this, "He welcomed the crowds and talked to them about the kingdom of God".

Why did he begin with teaching? Because as St John says in his Gospel (6, 26), without this teaching the crowds may think that this is just another miracle of ordinary bread, rather than a "sign" of the new age that Jesus is establishing. The individual and the community are oppressed by many different kinds of hunger. To be liberated from hunger, the individual and the community have to believe in Jesus, in a personal way. They have to get involved in his liberating and saving work. It is a mistake to begin by asking what I can get out of this celebration for myself. When St John says that the Eucharistic celebration is a "sign "of the new age, he certainly does not mean that we can privatise it.

Our school children can help us here perhaps. Children have great difficulty in trying to understand miracles today. But they are very interested in animals or children that are hungry. And starving! The children know that without food children die. They can understand that food gives life, when it is shared in a more or less equal way. Don't forget that St Luke is talking here about sharing bread.

Jesus is not saying that if the poor wait long enough, that they will get something to eat! To be credible, Jesus' liberation of the human family has to begin here and now. The kingdom that Jesus is preaching is very down to earth. It is not just about saving souls. The whole person and the community have to begin to be liberated and saved now.

St John's account of the feeding of the 5,000 tells us that this event is a "sign". A sign of what? A sign of Jesus' universal mission to liberate and save the human family, now and in the future, from hunger and all the other oppressive forces that devalue the human person and the community. Jesus cannot do this at a safe impersonal distance. He has to share his life with the individual and the community.

This means that the feeding of the 5,000 anticipates and foreshadows the new age when every family will have food. At this celebration, the people sat down in groups of fifty, as they would at a wedding feast.

This celebration also anticipates the Last Supper.

"Do you wish to honour the body of Jesus? Do not ignore him when he is naked. Do not pay him homage in the temple clad in silk, and then to neglect him when outside cold and hungry" (St John Chrysoston, 4th century).

Discussion Questions

Why do millions die of hunger today?

Why does the church celebrate the Eucharist?

Why do we use bread to celebrate the Eucharist?

What difference does the Eucharist make to the way that we love other people?

Why should a young disciple of Jesus spend time celebrating the Eucharist, when he could be out helping the poor?

Do we know the people who are hungry?

Is it all right to help the poor without loving them?

When do we meet Jesus in the street?

How can we demonstrate our belief in the Eucharist?

Season of Ordinary Time

2nd Sunday of the year
This was the first of the signs given by Jesus.
John 2: 1-12

The central issue here is not about the miracle of turning water into wine. St John talks more about what he calls "signs" than miracles. The marriage feast of Cana calls for a "quantum leap" in our human and religious understanding. In the Bible, the sacred and the religious come to us in a human way. If we devalue or disregard the human (as we are well inclined to do!), then the sacred and the religious will evaporate.

In the Old Testament, God was the Bridegroom of Israel. And Israel was the bride. To meet the bridegroom, Israel had to go to the temple in Jerusalem to hear the word of God and to pray. Once Jesus, the new Bridegroom had come, the sacred and the religious were more human and personal. The old temple was destroyed. And Jesus became the new temple, the new sacred place where God and the human community meet. In the Old Testament the Bridegroom was in heaven. Now, Jesus, the Bridegroom is here with us in a human and personal way.

At the wedding feast of Cana, Jesus has his disciples with him – which includes his mother. They are the beginning of a new Messianic people. St John says that when they saw the "sign", they believed in Jesus. The "sign" was the changing of the water into wine. The "sign" is a foreshadowing of Jesus' entire ministry. This marriage feast lacked wine. The water in the six water jars had to do with admission to the feast by purification. But it was totally inadequate (like the old Covenant that it represented) to prepare men for this feast. Yet it is this water that Jesus turns into wine. Now the wedding can go ahead, and foreshadow the final marriage between God and his people. John says that when the disciples saw the "sign" they believed in Jesus. That is a lot more demanding than just believing in the God of the Old Testament. Believing in Jesus means believing in his life and historical project to set the downtrodden free.

A disciple has to do more than tick boxes and commandments at a safe distance. A disciple has to enter, in a creative way, into the mystery of love, as Jesus understands it. With Jesus' help, a disciple has to turn water into wine!

"Go and preach, 'The kingdom of God is near!'. Heal the sick, raise the dead, make the lepers clean, drive out demons" (Matthew 10, 8).

Discussion Questions

In the Bible the sacred comes to us in a human way. Is that right?

Jesus became the new temple. What does that mean?

The sacred has become human. What does that tell us?

What did the water jars represent here?

The water turned into wine is a sign of what?

Does the church turn any water into wine today?

What was the significance of Mary's intervention?

What is the difference between a sign and a miracle?

3rd Sunday of the year
He has sent me to bring good news to the poor
Luke 1: 1-4, 4, 14-21

Guided by the Spirit, St Luke has to do more than tell the original Gospel story again. He has to interpret the Gospel for the wider Gentile Christian community. Luke begins with the incident at the Synagogue in Nazareth. "He places this incident at the beginning of Jesus' ministry in Galilee, because it gives us the pattern for Jesus' entire ministry. Led by the Spirit, Jesus now spells out the vision and mission of a Christian prophet". (La Verdiere).

Significantly, while St Mark opens his gospel account with a call to repentance because the Kingdom is close (1, 14), St Luke focuses on the call of the downtrodden to the kingdom of the Spirit.

In the Synagogue at Nazareth Jesus preaches from a text by the prophet Isaiah. He says that he has been sent to bring glad tidings to the poor. The poor are those who live in poverty, have no voice to speak for themselves and are oppressed by hunger, disease, lack of education. They suffer injustice at the hands of the people in power.

In the parable of the rich man and Lazarus (also by St Luke) Jesus tells us that he favours the poor not because they are moral or religious, but because they are only half human. And God cannot tolerate it. He takes it as a personal insult.

Western theology is slow in becoming aware of the full implication of the Incarnation. St John the evangelist tells us that once Jesus becomes man, the sacred moves from the Temple in Jerusalem to the body of Jesus (2, 21). and then every human person and the human community become Temples of Jesus and of God." You are the temple of God" (1Cor. 3, 16).

As I say, Western theology has difficulty with this. The roots of our academic theology do not go down very deep into the emotional depths of the human community. Consequently, the church's vision, at local level, tends to become professional. Jesus is not a professional man. He is fully human. He has an emotional bond with the poor that is fully human and personal. To liberate and save the human family, he has to risk his interior and exterior life. Next Sunday's gospel will explore this.

Discussion Questions

St Luke had to interpret the original gospel for the Gentile?.

Do we have to interpret anything for the modern secular world?

Why does St Luke begin his gospel with this incident in the synagogue in Nazareth?

Why does Jesus say that he is sent with glad tidings for the poor?

What is so special about the poor?

Do the poor help the rich in any way?

Do the poor have a moral or religious something that attracts Jesus?

Is the human person a temple of the Spirit?

Was the human person a temple of the Spirit before the Incarnation?

Does Jesus have an emotional bond with the poor?

4th Sunday of the year
Is not this the carpenter's son?
Luke 4: 21-30

St Mark says that Jesus was rejected at Nazareth at the end of his first year (6, 1). St Luke places this episode at the beginning of Jesus' ministry, because it announces the pattern that his ministry is to follow. At first Jesus got an enthusiastic reception, but suddenly mob violence erupted. Why? Because Jesus refuses to fall into line with the established religious order of the Jewish community. The people of Nazareth felt that they were the chosen People, and that Jesus' ministry should exclude the unwashed and unclean Gentiles. Jesus rubbed salt into their wounds by telling them stories of earlier Prophets who gave preferential treatment to pagans, at a time when members of the Jewish community were in dire need of help.

We need to remind ourselves here that Jesus belonged to the prophetic tradition. He begins his visit to Nazareth with "The Spirit of the Lord is upon me". Earlier St Luke told us that Jesus was baptized by the Holy Spirit. The Prophet represents the divine plan of liberation and salvation. And that plan is wider than any community that is already established. The Prophet, guided by the Spirit, does not allow the Jewish religious establishment (nor the Christian church) to settle down in a comfort zone. The point is that the well-heeled, once they get into power, tend to work on instinct only. Like wild life.

The faith and love that Jesus is promoting is wider than the family, the village, the tribe. Jesus wants the individual and the community to develop in a human and Christian way. As Fr Segundo says, "Self-giving is the most serious, demanding, unpredictable, irreversible adventure that can happen to a human being".

When we love somebody, we risk the deepest and most vulnerable part of ourselves, and we may get no response. By including the Gentiles in his ministry, Jesus risked mob violence, as all the Prophets in the Bible did. And Christian Prophets do today. Archbishop Romero would be an example today.

So why do the Prophets take the risk? Because when a community stops growing, it begins to go to seed. First, it loses the democratic ability to communicate with the human community. Then it may go on to claim all sorts of divine rights. Next it tends to go back to the instinctual level. But on the way back, it begins to lose the ability to believe and to love. At this point the poor are the first to suffer, because nobody sees the man who has fallen among robbers!

But the prophet is on watch. The Holy Spirit empowers the disciple of Jesus to take the risk, of following the human and Christian dream of love - a love that is not limited to prejudice or instinct. Then the individual and the community are empowered to take risks for the poor.

Discussion Questions

Why did mob violence erupt on this occasion?

Why did Jesus not play the game of the Jewish religious establishment on this occasion?

Jesus belongs to the Prophetic tradition. What is important about that?

Does the Prophet represent a divine plan that is always wider, and more evolved than the stage that the community is at?

Do people in power want to settle-down in a comfort zone?

Why do people who live in the past begin to lose their ability to believe and to love?

Can a disciple love without taking a risk?

What happens to the poor when people begin to lose their ability to love?

What is so important about the poor?

5th Sunday of the year
Put out into deep water
Luke 5:1-11

According to St Luke, Jesus calls his first disciples in an unlikely setting. It was not during a religious ceremony in the Synagogue, nor in the Temple glittering with gold. No. It was in the midst of a fishing community at their daily work. Fr Gutierrez says that the gospel must be preached where the human community is trying to build something that is more human.

Here Jesus has to borrow Peter's boat to use as a makeshift pulpit to teach the crowds about the new age of justice and love. Peter's call to be an apostle is inserted into Jesus' life and mission. Jesus also makes use of the fishermen's language. He says to Peter, "From now on, you'll catch people".

St Luke wants to tell us that a disciple is especially called by Jesus. He seems to be aware that the authority of the apostles needs to have solid foundations Why? Because the apostles were uneducated laymen. And yet their mission is worldwide (Luke himself had a Greek education.) This is highlighted by the miraculous catch of fish, which filled two boats to sinking point. The two boats may be an indication that the church is a community of mutual assistance, in the mission field.

Simon (or Peter) is now asked to put out into deep water, where the apostles failed to catch anything the night before. Does this mean that in our time the church has to engage in some sort of dialogue with the depth of the modern secular world? We are all becoming more aware that something needs to be done along these lines. It's the how to do it that scares us!

In the old days we had the impression that the church is perfect. That it had all the questions and all the answers ready made! If that happened to be the case, which it is not, being a Christian would be less of an adventure. And the individual disciple of Jesus would have a less creative role. The church would be very boring!

Vatican II tells us that the church is a leaven and a sort of soul for the human family. But the leaven is not ready-made, just like that.

The Council tells us that, "The church is joined to the rest of men in a search for truth (The Church Today, 16). It says that the church has to look for "Signs of God's presence and purpose, in the happenings, needs and desires in which this People has a part along with other men of our age" (The Church Today, 11).

In the gospel account that we are looking at, we can notice that Jesus had to borrow Simon's (or Peter's) boat, to use as a sort of pulpit. In evangelising the modern secular world, the clergy have to get used to working with the laity, because it is the laity who take the gospel to the family, the school, the place of work, the city and so on. But the laity cannot be sent out without what St Paul calls "The armour of Christ". They need an updated version of the life and mission of Jesus, and of the church. This means that the clergy and laity, at a local level, have to start evangelising each other, in small parish groups. This cannot be left to experts and theologians.

Why not? Because the local community has to make the gospel its own. Each person has to take personal responsibility for relating the gospel to the local culture. The gospel does not come alive until it passes through the humanity of the local community. It has to reach the deepest emotional level of the local community.

Discussion Questions

Why did Jesus call the Apostles while they were at work?

Does the church have any interest in the places where people work today?

Why did Jesus use Peter's boat and the language of the fishermen?

What language does the church use today?

Does the church need the help of the human community today?

How is the church, "Joined with the rest of mankind in the search for truth"?

Are there any signs of God's presence in the human community today?

Are all the church's questions and answers (in its dialogue with the world) ready-made by the church itself?

Does the church have something to learn from dialogue with the human community today?

6th Sunday of the year
The sermon on the plain
Luke 6:17, 20-26

St Luke is dealing with the beatitudes here. The scripture experts say that St Luke's and St Matthew's accounts of the beatitudes are, to some extent, expanding on an earlier written version of the gospel. A gospel that we know about only because St Luke and St Matthew are giving us parts of it. All the gospel writers are, of course, guided by the Spirit of Jesus. It is the way that the two Evangelists (Matthew and Luke) differ from each other that is fascinating. The Christian community has a creative role in presenting the gospel in a way that is geared to local communities. This is a challenge for the church today.

In St Matthew's account of the Beatitudes, Jesus is talking to a select number of disciples on a mountain. They are to continue Jesus' liberating and saving work. St Luke pictures Jesus coming down from a mountain to the plain. The twelve disciples are still there, but now they are joined by a large crowd from all over Judea and Jerusalem, and the seacoast of Tyre and Sidon. Luke wants to indicate that Jesus' historical project is universal.

St Luke retains much of Jesus' original passionate, human, personal, urgent (eschatological) aspects of Jesus' original beatitudes. This is a moment of grace that calls out for an urgent response from the Christian and human communities. In Jesus a new age has arrived. "It opens to human existence a new hope that transcends 'this life'" (Gutierrez).

Luke's Beatitudes include four beatitudes for the poor and four woes for the rich. The poor, the hungry, those who weep and are persecuted are blessed, because they now have somebody to speak for them and to fight their battles. On the other hand, the rich people who are laughing and happy now, are reminded that this is one of the most solemn events in the gospel and in their lives. They are called to repent. Now. Today.

The rich make an important contribution to the community and to the poor. The rich make a huge contribution to the liberation of the poor. They lead the way in providing food and medicine (In Europe at least we all live longer!). The rich also make a big contribution to human rights.

But sadly it remains the case, even today, that the poor are often not allowed to speak for themselves. Consequently, they do not always have the freedom to come to Jesus, and to each other, in a personal way. Jesus wants every person to become more human, because he wants to share his human and divine life with us – in a personal way. Without freedom and equality it is very difficult to love.

We cannot become free ourselves unless we are promoting the freedom of other people.

Discussion Questions

Why are we given different versions of the gospel?

Why is it that in St Luke the beatitudes are announced to a large crowd?

Why does St Luke not choose the mountain setting for the beatitudes?

Why does St Luke retain much of the personal and social urgency of the original beatitudes?

Is this a solemn moment in the gospel?

Why are Jesus and St Luke so kind to the poor here?

What are Jesus and St Luke saying to the rich here?

Why should everybody have the right to speak for themselves?

How is freedom related to love?

How does this gospel help the church today?

7th Sunday of the year
Love your enemies
Luke 6: 27-38

Here St Luke is setting out the new law of Jesus Christ. "Love your enemies. If a man slaps you on one cheek, present the other cheek too". In a highly competitive capitalist culture like ours, Jesus' beatitudes appear, at first sight, like a useful lesson only for Sunday school children!

Many Christians today have not been through a personal conversion. As St Paul says to the Corinthians "I had to speak to you as infants in Christ. I fed you with milk, not solid food, for you were not ready for solid food. Even now you are still not ready" (1Cor. 3, 2). What I'm trying to say is that Jesus' beatitudes are rolled out for everybody. But to really understand the Beatitudes, our faith needs to move to an adult level. What does that mean? Before Jesus sends us out to love our enemies, he gives us a new commandment that we should love one another as he loved us first.

Our problem today is that many of us are cradle Catholics. We don't ask questions. We let other people do it for us! Jesus says that the kingdom of heaven is like a man who found a treasure in a field; he had to sell all he had to buy the field, and then dig up the treasure. Jesus is talking about a personal conversion. "The kingdom of heaven is like a treasure hidden in a field, which someone found and hid. Then in his joy he goes off, sells all he has and buys the field" (Matthew 13, 44).

Before we can love our enemies, Jesus invites us to break out of our capitalist mind-set What is a capitalist mind-set? A capitalist is someone who possesses his dog, his wife, his children, his house, his mortgage and himself. The more baggage he has, the more real he feels. He tends to identify himself with his possessions. These possessions have to be protected by gates, dogs, insurance and electronic stuff. He is afraid to share. To become human we have to share with other people. That is why Jesus, in the Beatitudes, invites us to allow him to come to us, in a personal way, and share his life. To a large extent, Jesus remains a stranger until we get personally involved in his mission. What mission? To liberate the downtrodden from the many oppressive forces (most of them well and truly hidden) that keep the individual sub-human. Jesus remains a stranger until we begin to announce Jesus' message of human rights, justice, equality, freedom and community.

None of this will appear real until we start to do it. Once we start to remove the chains from other persons, our own chains (capitalist chains that we did not even notice before) will begin to fall away. Then the mystery of love takes over.

To continue on this pilgrim way, we usually need the support of a community. We need the community to listen with us to the word of Jesus, and translate it into a language that makes sense in the modern world.

Discussion Questions

Is Jesus asking too much here?

What is a cradle Catholic?

What is a personal conversion?

What is an adult Christian?

What is a capitalist mind-set?

To become human or Christian, we have to share with other people. Why?

Why do we have to get personally involved in Jesus' mission?

What is Jesus' mission today?

Why don't we notice our own chains, until we help to remove the chains of other people?

How does the word of Jesus help?

8th Sunday of the year
A fully trained disciple has to be like his master.
Luke 6:39-45

Our first temptation here will be to think that Jesus is thinking of the person who lives next door to me. The one that I cannot get on with! I don't think that Jesus is thinking exclusively of that person, because a disciple has responsibility for everybody in the human and Christian families. Everybody is my brother and sister.

A lot of disciples today seem to be passive and resigned to the blind, domineering and oppressive forces that we all meet today in the secular city, and sometimes, let us face it, in the Christian community too. We know that there are people out there struggling for human rights, children's rights, equality, freedom, and the rights of the poor and so on. Meanwhile, our spirituality is to be too dependent on prayer to solve everything. It solves a lot of things, but not everything.

I hasten to add that the negative note above is not the whole story. A lot of wonderful things also happen in the margins of the human and Christian communities. In the Old Testament the prophets ministered in the margins of the community. And Jesus is found there too. As well as in the mainstream today, there are life-forces at work in the margins of the Christian community. These people feel that to rediscover the mystery of Jesus today (a mystery which includes his historical project), they have to go back to Jesus himself and listen to his word. Very often they feel that they have to listen to the word together, as a community. It is the community, supporting each other, that gets rid of the splinters and planks in the eye. And worse! The fear that does not allow us to take a look in the mirror!

This new life-force, inside or outside the mainstream, is called evangelisation. The individual disciple discovers himself or herself in his or her encounter with his neighbour. He learns to stop being afraid and to come out and take a risk - the risk of hope and the risk of love. It is when we get involved in the struggle to set others free, that we discover what Jesus is talking about.

"In the evangelists' accounts, Jesus was not born in a "house" but in a stable, and among beasts. His birth is witnessed by the marginalised: shepherds and itinerant Oriental magi. When he is brought to the temple, only two marginalised grasp the importance of his coming life. Unlike his contemporaries he does not marry. He enrols in none of the theological schools. He prefers the company of fishers and other folk of humble social standing. His concern is for the popular masses, the rejected by the dominant society" (Hoornaert).

Discussion Questions

Does a disciple have some responsibility for the oppressive forces that stalk the secular city today?

Are we too dependent on faith without good works?

Do we have responsibility for promoting human rights?

Why did the Old Testament prophets live on the margins of the community?

What life-forces are at the work in the margins of the Christian community today?

How can we get to know Jesus today?

Why do we need other people to listen to the word of Jesus with us?

The individual encounters himself in his encounter with his neighbour? He also discovers the planks in his eyes?

Do we have to risk something in our encounters with other people?

9th Sunday of the year
Not even in Israel have I found faith like this
Luke 7:1-10

Here St Luke is focussing on Jesus' mission to the Gentiles. Jesus has already announced his mission to the Gentiles, in the synagogue at Nazareth (Luke 4, 25). The focus now is on the faith of a Gentile soldier, a centurion. The centurions (who commanded 100 men) were the backbone of the Roman army. They were long-serving regular soldiers. Capernaum had a military garrison made up of Syrian Gentiles. The fact that this centurion built the local synagogue suggests that he had certain solidarity with the Jewish faith and the Jewish people. The higher morality of the Jewish people would be attractive to the higher ranks of the Roman army.

But to believe in Jesus, the centurion had to go through a quantum-leap of personal faith. Because a person who believes in Jesus has also to believe in the historical mission of Jesus, to set the downtrodden free - beginning here and now. The centurion believed that Jesus could cure his servant with just a word. Jesus said that he had not found faith like that in Israel.

In his account of this event, St Matthew (8, 5) expands on this encounter. Jesus says that his encounter with the centurion foreshadows a new age when gentiles from east and west will come to Jesus and take their places in the kingdom, while the heirs to the kingdom will be thrown out.

St Matthew intends the community that he is writing for to take this as a warning. Belief in Jesus is a struggle because "Christian faith sustains itself by listening to the saving and creative word of Jesus" (Kapam).

In a complicated place such as the modern city, with its television stations communicating with every Christian living room, the disciple needs the support of a community who are listening to the word in a personal and creative way. This is not easy to do in a large impersonal community, which helps to explain the small marginal communities that are springing up in Parishes.

Discussion Questions

Who were the Gentiles?

Any Gentiles about today?

What was different about the faith of the Gentile soldier?

Is it harder to believe in Jesus than to believe in God?

Did the centurion believe in Jesus' historical mission?

In St Matthew does the centurion's faith foreshadow the entry of the Gentiles to the kingdom?

Is there a warning for the Christian church here?

How does faith grow?

Is it easy to believe in Jesus today?

10th Sunday of the year
Do not weep.
Luke 7: 11-17

This is a Jewish event that tells us something about Jesus, the Jewish community and the church. As Jesus approaches the city of Naim, he meets a widow who is crying. Her only son has died, and besides, she is a widow. She is accompanied by a large crowd of mourners. The weeping, silent widow, her son and the crowd, suggest that they represent the Jewish community at the time, and especially the plight of the common people.

Originally, Israel's religion was a religion of the common people. But after the shock of the exile of the community to Babylon, the professionals (Scribes, Pharisees and Sadducees) took over. The Prophets said that the exile was due to sin, but the professionals said that the common people ("Who did not know the Law"!) were the biggest sinners.

The common people were now reduced to tears (like the widow here). The flame of faith and hope was burning low, because the common people had no Prophet to speak for them. This helps to explain why it was that St Luke highlights the words of the people who have seen Jesus' sign (or miracle), "A great Prophet has risen among us. God has visited his people".

Don't forget that the widow's only son was dead. This suggests that the future of the community was at risk. The community as a whole was not well disposed towards Jesus. Communities that fail to move forward, who fail to catch the tide (as Shakespeare says), are in danger of losing what they have achieved so far.

Here we can see how human Jesus is. He enters into solidarity with a community that is distressed because it has no voice and no Prophet to speak for it. St Luke says that Jesus was "Deeply moved" when he saw the widow. He said to her, "Do not weep". And to her son, "Young man, I say to you, rise. The dead man sat up and began to speak".

"Jesus raises us up and makes us speak. It is a goodness that has historical implications and effects. Luke does not forget a very human detail about Jesus: "He gave him to his mother". (Gutierrez).

Discussion Questions

Who or what does the widow and her son represent?

The widow has no voice and her only son is dead. What does that tell us?

Why is Jesus "deeply moved" here?

Is the church deeply moved today?

Why does Jesus tell the widow not to weep?

Is Jesus' word life-giving today?

The widow's son is able to speak. Does that have any significance?

Why does St Luke celebrate the presence of, "A great Prophet" here?

Does Jesus have a mission to give life?

11th Sunday of the year
Jesus took him up and said, Simon I have something to say to you
Luke 7: 36-8, 3

Here St Luke invites us to take a closer look at the mystery of repentance and forgiveness. The woman at the centre of the drama here is a public sinner, who is socially and religiously despised and marginalised. The Pharisee, who represents the religious establishment, can do nothing constructive for the woman.

St Luke tells us that the woman treats Jesus as a Lord, and believes in him as a Lord. But she also has to love him. We should not imagine that all that Jesus has to do is "Wipe the slate clean" (Fr Gutierrez). A public sinner is a stranger to the community. Before he returned home, the Prodigal Son was dining with the pigs in an unclean and foreign land!

So Jesus has to build a bridge across the chasm that separates the woman from himself. As Lord, he is able to bridge the chasm, but St Luke is very clear that Jesus needs to approach this woman as a human being. With a love that is fully human. That is why St Luke uses the name Jesus, when Jesus is talking to the woman.

Why is that important? This woman has lost part of her humanity, and consequently, part of her confidence in herself to respond to Jesus and to make the perilous journey through the road-blocks, and the pain-barriers, that stands between her and Jesus.

Jesus has to come to the woman in a very human way. When children are in trouble, they want to touch their parents physically. Jesus has to let her wash his feet. Jesus has to act as the Good Shepherd. He has to take responsibility for the woman's life, until she is on safe ground again. Jesus has to help this woman to rebuild her humanity. Repentance and forgiveness is not just a matter of words. It is a new creation. Without his human presence and support, she would not have the energy to accept his love and forgiveness.

And then Jesus goes on to say an amazing thing! That the people, who are forgiven the most, will have the greater love! Presumably, because the people who have been forgiven the most, have had the most love lavished on them by Jesus and God.

Discussion Questions

What is a public sinner?

The woman treats Jesus as a Lord. What does that tell us?

Why does St Luke say that it was the human Jesus that spoke to the woman?

Is there more to repentance and forgiveness than "Wiping the slate clean"?

How far away from Jesus are public sinners?

Had this woman lost part of her humanity?

Are repentance and forgiveness a new creation?

Is there a pain-barrier involved in repentance?

Is it easy to forgive people today?

Is it easy to repent today?

Does the church need to approach the Sacrament of reconciliation in a more human way today?

12th Sunday of the year
Who do you say that I am?
Luke 9:18-24

Here Jesus asks the Apostle, "Who do the crowds say that I am?" This question is important, because Jesus' mission is universal, and also because what the crowds are saying tells us something of what they have been told (or not told) about Jesus. The crowds are saying that Jesus is one of the ancient Prophets. "Ancient" is added by St Luke himself, to the parallel gospel accounts.

This puts mileage between Jesus and the ancient Prophets. This is another way of saying that the Apostles (and the church) cannot bask in the warm glow, or hide behind, the established political or religious orders. A disciple has to stand up and be counted.

A major part of Jesus' mission has to do with liberating the human family from the oppressive forces (hunger, disease, injustice) that keeps it in chains. This cannot be done by ducking and diving and focussing on personal survival regardless of the cost to the Christian and human communities. In fact, St Luke wants to save Peter's blushes here, by bypassing a sharp exchange between Jesus and Peter that St Matthew carries in the parallel account (Matthew 16, 22). Peter was advising Jesus that the cross was a bad idea! Jesus said to Peter, "Get behind me, Satan"! That is strong language for St Matthew, who likes to say nice things about the Apostles.

In our time, each individual disciple of Jesus has to answer for himself or herself. In the past we tended to leave it to the community. Today the individual disciple lives in a competitive society. Our family, our tribe and our community cannot take all the big decisions for us. This helps to explain the following statement by Fr Karl Rahner: "The future of the church in Germany cannot be planned and built up merely by the application of generally recognised Christian principles. It needs the courage of an ultimately charismatically inspired, creative imagination"

(The Shape of the Church to Come, 47).

Discussion Questions

Is what the crowds are saying about Jesus important?

Why does St Luke add "ancient" to the original, found in St Mark?

Can the apostles bask on the warm glow of the ancient Prophets?

Can the church today bask in the glow of its sacred traditions?

What does it mean to hide behind the established order (political or religious)?

Does part of Jesus' mission have to do with liberating the oppressed?

Why is Peter reluctant to follow Jesus' way?

How is Jesus' cross and resurrection related to his saving plan?

13th Sunday of the year
I will follow you wherever you go
Luke 9: 51-62

Individual Samaritans, Pharisees and Romans did welcome Jesus. But established communities of the Samaritans, Pharisees and Romans did not welcome him, though Jesus did preach to their communities to start with. Communities (political or religious) tend to be founded by charismatic individuals, individuals who have a dream of a more human way of life. But the struggle to keep the community together over a long period of time can easily tend to give the community a hard, legalistic and unattractive edge.

Jesus respected the communities of the time, but he did not want to become too dependent on them. And so to one would-be disciple Jesus says, "Foxes have holes and the birds of the air have nests, but the Son of Man has nowhere to lay his head" (Luke 9, 58).

Jesus' way of life was (humanly) attractive to individuals emerging from the established communities - especially younger folk. Younger people often want to test the boundaries of the communities that they belong to. Younger people, at the time, saw Jesus as the young Prophet from Galilee, who was promoting the original dream of the People of God. What dream? The dream to promote a more human community based on justice, freedom and human rights.

The community that Jesus is offering to his disciples is different. It is not entirely ready-made and pre-packaged. That is the type of community that children need and want. Jesus offers his disciple a creative freedom and a mission to, "open the eyes of the blind, set the downtrodden free, and announce Glad Tidings to the poor". This is attractive to young people or to people with a young and flexible mind-set, who are overcoming their fear of stepping outside their comfort zone. But a lot of people will find this journey from their old established communities more than challenging. "Another to whom Jesus said, 'Follow me' replied, "Let me go and bury my father first" (Lk.9, 60). Another would-be disciple wanted time to say goodbye to his friends!

To become a disciple, a person has to break the compulsions that tie him to his family, class, tribe, city, culture, colour, traditions, history, male and female. These bonds are not devalued, quite the reverse. They are given a new orientation, as they become part of the mystery of the life and mission of Jesus.

St Luke is telling us here that Jesus is on his last journey to Jerusalem. The dream of building a more human community is a very expensive one. But Jesus does not suffer alone. He suffers in solidarity with the poor and downtrodden. Ultimately, it is love that makes the Christian life possible.

"Our present situation is one of transition from a church sustained by a unified Christian society and almost identical with it. From a people's church, to a church made up of those who have struggled against their environment, in order to reach a personally clearly and explicitly responsible decision of faith". Emphasis added. (Fr Karl Rahner, the Future of the Church 24).

Discussion Questions

Why do communities tend to lose their enthusiasm as time goes on?

What kind of people did Jesus attract in his time –young old, rich or poor?

Why did Jesus say that foxes have holes…?

Why did Jesus not get personally involved in the religious or political communities of the time?

Why do young people want to test the boundaries of their communities?

Was Jesus seen as a Prophet?

Does Jesus offer us a creative part in his community today?

Do the individuals who come to Jesus have a mission to build a more human community, and a more human world?

14th Sunday of the year
Carry no purse, no haversack, no sandals
Luke 10: 1-12, 17-20

St Luke says that the kingdom, the new age, is brought near in the coming of Jesus. And it will be extended by his disciples. The kingdom is present now in Jesus and his disciples. It is a kingdom of justice, equality, freedom. The disciples will have no time for "Time-consuming futilities and wayside etiquette" (Caird). The kingdom has to be grasped when the opportunity arises. The opportunity can be lost. Remember the cities that Jesus wept over! Whoever rejects the disciple rejects Jesus as well.

St Luke says that the disciples are to carry no baggage (purse, haversack, sandals). Being poor does not, in itself, guarantee anything. If poverty was enough, there would be little point in helping the poor. The point being made is that the disciples have to give up the usual safe mooring in this world. The disciples will be tempted by the securities that money and power bring. They will be tempted to be on good terms with the keepers of the establishment. The danger here is that they (and today's disciples) may barter away the right to question the goings on in the established order. The result would be Christianity without Jesus and the cross.

A Christianity without Jesus is a real temptation today. It is especially easy to lose touch with the humanity of Jesus, and our own humanity. A leading Latin American theologian (Fr Segundo S.J.), tells us that "In Latin America, we have one of the most Christian lands in the world, and one of the most inhuman".

How would a renewed focus on the humanity of Jesus help us today? The church's mission has to do with setting the downtrodden free and bringing Glad Tidings to the poor. If the church keeps to itself, and fails to help the man who has fallen among robbers, where is it going to meet Jesus in his humanity? We can't just say we'll meet him in the Eucharist. Because St John says in effect (1John 4:20) that if we bypass the man who has fallen among robbers, how will we recognise Jesus in the Eucharist?

Discussion Questions

Why do the disciples have no time to waste?

Can the opportunity to come to Jesus be lost?

Why must the disciples carry no baggage (purse, haversack etc.)?

Is being poor a guarantee of being a disciple?

How does being poor help evangelisation?

Why might the disciples want to keep on good terms with the established powers?

Do the disciples need the freedom to question in a critical way, the social and political powers?

What is a Christian community without the cross?

Why are the disciples like lambs among wolves?

15th Sunday of the year
Who is my neighbour?
Luke 10: 25-37

The Lawyer here wanted to win eternal life by a meticulous observance of religious laws and commandments. He was looking for a more scientific definition of what constitutes a neighbour, so that he could reduce his liabilities and responsibilities for his neighbour before God. God for him was a sort of cosmic policeman, with a short temper!

The lawyers at the time endlessly debated the kinds of people who could be excluded from the troublesome commandment to love your neighbour! Gentiles, maybe? Or the Samaritans? Or the lepers? In his letter to the Galatians, St Paul, the former Pharisee, says that all these debates about defining the Law are childish. A child needs a lot of clear rules and commandments, because he or she is not empowered to take personal responsibility for himself and the community.

Jesus is not interested in legalistic escapism. The parable of the Good Samaritan is designed to break the legalistic spell. The two professionals in the religious Law (the Priest and the Levite) failed to help the man who fell among robbers. Meanwhile, it was the despised Samaritan, who lacked the Lawyer's learning and fanatical obsession with security (the man on the roadside may be dead, or part of a plot to rob travellers), who has the secret of eternal life. The Samaritan approached the injured man in a really human way. He had compassion. And that was not just an empty feeling. It was a compassion that resulted in solidarity and action. He healed the man's wounds, and took the man to the Inn.

Jesus' Law is a law of faith and love. Jesus' community has to stop being afraid of everything and carrying loads of guilt. Legalism has to be kept on the back burner. Legalism is a burden that the human and Christian community cannot afford to carry. "Why do you now want to put God to the test by laying a load on the backs of believers which neither our ancestors nor we ourselves were able to carry?" (Acts15:10) The community has to save its energy to do battle for justice, freedom, human rights and love. Jesus' new law of love puts the rights of the individual person and the community of persons at the top of the church's agenda. The church is a servant of humanity.

The Good Samaritan went to work alone. We still need to work alone at times, because many people today fall among robbers. But as more and more injured people are difficult to locate (they may be hidden next door, or in our own house!), Vatican II reminds us that we need to work as a community. We need the wisdom of the community, because in our complex society it is difficult to distinguish between the people who genuinely need our help and those who are faking injury.

Discussion Questions:

What was the Lawyer up to here?

Why was the Lawyer so keen on the Law?

Was the Lawyer's God a legalist?

Why does St Paul say that it is children who need a lot of ready-made commandments?

Why did the Priest and the Levite fail to help the injured man?

The Samaritan was, "Moved with compassion". What does that tell us?

Are we ever "Moved with compassion" today?

Why do we need a community approach to love today?

Do more people fake injury or need today?

Is it sometimes difficult to locate the people who are falling among robbers today?

16th Sunday of the year
Mary has chosen the better part
Luke 10: 38-42

Martha is a very caring housewife. She is anxious about the physical needs of Jesus and her guests. But she is far too busy to see the big picture. She has not yet discovered what St Paul was to discover later "If I have faith to move mountains, but do not have love, I am nothing. And if I give away all my possessions, and if I hand over my body so that I may boast, but do not have love, I gain nothing" (1Cor. 13, 2).

We are told that Martha's sister, Mary, "Sat at Jesus' feet and listened to his word". Fr Gutierrez (Peru) tells us that "In Jesus' day, teachers of the law decided that it was not the place of women to delve into the teachings of God's law. This was the task and responsibility of men. With the Lord's approval, Mary is breaking that rule. Sitting at the Lord's feet (v. 39), she claims a right as a human person: to know directly, from the lips of Jesus, "mysteries hidden throughout the ages" (Col 1,26), the right to be a disciple".

In effect, Jesus is telling Martha, in a very gentle way, that she is a prisoner of a tradition that has passed its sell-by date. A tradition that would keep women as mere housewives, partly excluded from the Christian mission and responsibility to become human and Christian. That is not enough for Christian discipleship.

Jesus is a friend of Martha and Mary. "This friendship enables these women, and any woman, to find themselves as persons" (Gutierrez). With Martha and Mary, Jesus is not emphasising the institutional aspect of the church.

This helps to explain why the church today is trying to rediscover itself as a pilgrim church - a church of self-discovery at the level of baptism. At the level of baptism, all members of the church have equal rights and equal responsibilities. Without the freedom that equality gives, it is very difficult to love other people in a fully human and Christian way. For example, if you live in a castle with locked gates and dogs patrolling your ground and I'm a poor person living outside your gates, where is the equality and the love going to come from? At church on Sunday?

Jesus expects the individual and the community to dismantle their defence mechanisms and begin to take other people seriously and to take the mission of Jesus seriously. Jesus' love is designed to stretch the heart of the individual as well as the hearts of the human and Christian communities. To promote equality, justice, freedom, human and democratic rights and Christian rights.

Discussion Questions

Why was Martha worried?

Why did Martha not sit with Mary at the Lord's feet for a while?

Is it easy to combine the active ministry of the church today, with listening to the word of Jesus?

In the Old Testament, why were women not encouraged to "delve into the mystery of the word of God"?

Why did Jesus encourage Mary to move towards a new model of human and Christian responsibility?

Can the church today learn anything from this gospel?

What is wrong with being a mere housewife today?

Does the church need an adult membership today?

Why do the human and Christian communities have to struggle for justice and love today?

17th Sunday of the year
Ask and it will be given to you
Luke 11: 1-13

The basic questions about the church's prayer life go back to Scripture, and Jesus himself. But this prayer has been developed by the church over the years. The great Cathedrals, the monasteries and the convents, contributed quite a lot. In the old days, when education was limited, most individuals and communities were happy to use the ready-made prayers that had been handed down.

For our young people, it is somewhat different today. Why? Because we live in a competitive culture, where our children are educated to compete and to defend their human dignity, as well as their human and Christian rights. Our young disciples of Jesus want to bring this new outlook to their prayer life. They want to be able to play a creative role in the human and Christian Communities. These new disciples of Jesus want to do more than recite prayers in a mechanical and impersonal way. They want to come to Jesus; they want to pray, in a more personal way. As I say, these young people want to come to Jesus himself, as the apostles did in this gospel, and to be able to say to him "Lord, teach us how to pray".

Older disciples like you and I (!) tend to think of Jesus as God, without more ado. With the result that Jesus' humanity gets pushed into the background. This is most unhelpful to younger people. It's a disaster! They want to come to Jesus the human being, the Son of Mary, first! Why is that? Because they are more and more aware of the value of their own humanity. They want to become human. They spend days and weeks and years. They spend money and time, and any amount of pain (fasting and what-not) making themselves presentable and competitive. They are dimly aware that without Jesus, the human being, they will not be able to get to know God as a father who wants to come close to us in a human and personal way. Someone who wants to love us.

Here in St Luke's Gospel, Jesus talks about his father and our father, in a family setting. He uses the children's word, "Abba", for God the

Father. Jesus says that we should first pray for the community. Pray that the Father's kingdom should come. That is a kingdom of justice and love. This is the guideline for all prayer. It stops us, for example, for praying for something that might burden our neighbour. Then we can pray to Jesus (and with Jesus) for our individual needs. He told us to ask and keep asking. He expects us to believe that he will always answer our prayers, though he may delay until the time is right.

Discussion Questions

Did the old Cathedral, monastery and convent have a role in developing the Church's prayer Life?

Were they happy with ready-made prayers in the old days?

Why are our young people less interested in ready-made prayers today?

Does competitive education make a difference to the way that young people pray?

Why do our young people want to pray in a more personal way?

Why should we pray for the coming of the kingdom?

Does Jesus promise to answer our prayers?

Do we have to believe that our prayers will always be answered?

18th Sunday of the year
A man's life is not made secure by what he owns.
Luke 12: 13-21

The man with the question here represents the crowds. The crowds are worried about security, and material possessions seem to promise that security. St Luke is telling us that the Christian community is in danger from the same temptations.

The mere possession of riches is not the problem for the Christian community. The problem is that riches cast a spell on the rich man. He becomes like a rabbit caught in the headlights of a car at night.

He starts to build bigger barns, and gates, and castles with moats. Dogs start to patrol his lawn; ground-to-air missiles protect his tribe. And when he gets pathologically bored, as he will do, he may think that it's time to start a war or something exciting! He may well belong to a class of people who, in the words of Jesus, "Tie up heavy burdens, hard to bear, and lay them on the shoulders of others" (Matthew 23, 4). He has a phoney understanding of human development.

The rich man's problem is that he is losing touch with the human community, and with his own humanity. He only talks to himself! "I will say to my soul …take things easy, eat, drink and have a good time" (Lk.12, 19). Once this happens, he may be afraid to go out to meet the human community. Yet nothing else will cure him. He needs to get involved in the community to promote justice, freedom and human rights. To become human himself he has to get involved in the struggle, to promote the humanity of other people. Human development cannot be bought for gold, or won in the national lottery. Where do these Christian temptations towards insecurity and greed come from?

At times the church can give the impression that Jesus' kingdom of justice and love are a religious dream, rather than something that can and must start to become a reality right now. Something that any disciple can and should have a creative role in helping to bring about. The Christian community and the individual disciple must have a mission, a historical project to humanise and evangelise.

Again, a disciple cannot begin to promote Jesus' kingdom of justice and love on his or her own. He needs the support of a community, especially today when the Christian way of life is often challenged by the crowds of spin-doctors and celebrities that control the television stations. They tend to tell us that to be a celebrity we have to win the national lottery

Discussion Questions

Can riches cast a spell on people today?

What is so important about being in touch with the human community?

Can we become real without the help of the human community?

Can we get to Jesus while bypassing the human community?

Why did the rich man talk to himself?

Why do rich people have a lot of security – gates and alarms etc.?

To become human himself, does the rich person have to get involved in the struggle to liberate other people?

Is the Christian way of life challenged by anybody today?

Is the Christian community aware of its down-to-earth historical mission today?

What is the mission of the church today?

19th Sunday of the year
My master is taking his time coming
Luke 12: 32-48

Jesus tells the disciple that even though they are only a "Little flock", with no fearsome defence capability, they are not to be afraid. Why not? Because the Father has given them the life and mission of Jesus. And Jesus himself. That is the kingdom. A kingdom of justice and love.

The community is not to worry about the many members of the human community who are not, physically, in the church. The church is at the service of the human family. By promoting justice and love in the human community, the church is helping the human community to become aware that it is beginning to live the life of Jesus. The church tells us that the Christian community is the soul of humanity (Vatican II, The Church Today, 40 and 22).

While time and history lasts, the church has responsibility for witnessing to the kingdom of Jesus at the heart of the human community. This means that the church has to "Keep watch" for the oppressive forces that stalk the human and Christian communities. The oppressor will bypass the bleeding man on the road. He will not notice people who are hungry and naked, because he has more exciting things to think about. He has built a bigger barn and is trying to get it filled before the winter! While "watching", the disciples have to "Keep their lamps lit". The lamp of the Christian community is the word of Jesus, the gospel.

It is the community that must hear the gospel in the first place. Normally, the members of the community must support each other while listening to the word, because no individual has all the gifts of the Spirit - the gifts of the Spirit have to be shared. Otherwise the "lamp" of the community can grow dim.

The individual disciple can hear the gospel on his or her own, but normally it is the community that interprets the gospel, and relates it to what Vatican II calls "The signs of the times".

Then St Luke deals with the servants who are in charge of the community. Jesus calls them "The stewards that the master has placed over his household". Most Biblical commentators think that in St Luke's experience, some of the leaders of the church are letting the Christian community down. They are not taking care of the sheep. They appear to be exploiting the community ("Beating the menservants and the maids, and getting drunk").

It would appear that the "lamps" that the community leaders are using are running low in oil. They are not listening to the word of Jesus. Consequently, they are lacking in a personal faith and love. They need to rediscover the personal presence of Jesus and his Holy Spirit here and now. The community will help them, if it is allowed.

Discussion Questions

Why might the "little flock" be afraid?

How does the church overcome its fear?

How do the disciples become servants of the human community today?

The church has to "watch" on its own behalf, and on behalf of the human community. What does that mean?

How do the disciples "keep their lamps lit"?

How can the community hear the word of Jesus in a creative way?

How do the gifts of the Spirit help the community to hear the word of Jesus in a creative way?

St Luke says that some church leaders let the church down. How?

Do any church leaders let the community down today?

20th Sunday of the year
I have not come to bring peace but division.
Luke 12: 49-53

Jesus now says that his gospel will bring division in the human family and the human community. Or it will bring to light the divisions that are already there, but hidden from the man and woman in the street. Some people will be for the gospel, others will cling to their comfort zones, clinging desperately to the old securities.

In the old days, we had a tendency to believe that all a disciple has to do is follow the community and do what he was told. And take little responsibility for human and Christian development. That worked in the old days because the individual and the community did not have to compete, with the secular world, as much as we have to compete today – with a television set in every Christian living room – and the Internet, telling us what to think and say and do!

In today's gospel, Jesus seems to be indicating that his disciples will have to do more than follow the crowd. They will have to be involved in personal battles, even within their own families, to hold on to Jesus and to take his gospel of justice and love into the heart of the human community, where there are many competing beliefs.

The individual disciple today is called to play a personal and creative role in building (with Jesus) a more human family and community. A community that promotes justice and peace, freedom and human rights. This cannot be done in a Christian way without a personal love for Jesus and his gospel. Without his gospel, we would have little idea about the mystery of justice and love.

Fr Comblin (a Latin American theologian on social justice) tells us: "Jesus' opponents were not common criminals, well known reprobates, public delinquents. Quite the contrary, they were pillars of the community, honourable people, respected and respectable. They did not reject Jesus or abuse him because they were base, ignorant, and immoral by community standards, but precisely because they were the acknowledged learned and virtuous members of the community. Their objections proceeded not from social weakness but from social strength mobilized to defend their false ideology and egoism. None of us can feel safe from this danger".

Discussion Questions

Is there such a thing as a false peace?

Why does Jesus attack a false peace?

Any false peace about today?

Should we just follow the community and not ask questions?

Does a disciple have to take some responsibility for human and Christian development today?

Does the Christian community have to compete with the secular world today?

Does the Christian community have to promote justice as well as peace today?

How does Jesus help us to promote justice today?

What kind of people were opposed to Jesus and his gospel?

21st Sunday of the year
Strive to enter by the narrow door
Luke 13: 22-30

Jesus does not respond directly to the question about the numbers who will be saved. Why not? Because it is idle speculation and a distraction from the kingdom of justice and love that Jesus is here to roll-out right now. Legalism and institutional fixes are very attractive to some members of every religious and human community. Partly because they are necessary, but also because they offer a hidden escape from personal commitment. Jesus says that the individual disciple cannot just follow the crowd or the tribe into the kingdom. He or she has to "strive" to enter by the narrow door. Here the word "strive" is taken from the original "agony" which suggests some degree of violence!

At an Oriental festival or wedding, worshippers, guests, spectators and gate-crashers, often had to fight their way through narrow doors, doors that would not remain open indefinitely. It is not being suggested that a disciple should try to get through the narrow door on his or her own. That is the last thing that they should try!

The point is that the individual disciple should, at the start, make a personal commitment to Jesus' one commandment - to love - to love him personally. Without this over-arching commandment, all the other rules and commandments get distorted. In the Parable of the Prodigal Son, for example, the Eldest Son has kept all his father's commandments, but he does not appear to love anybody. He says to his father, "I have slaved for you"! St Paul reminds us that if he gave all his goods to feed the poor, but was lacking in love, it would do him no good.

Jesus says that the narrow door will not stay open indefinitely. And it is not acceptable to arrive late with lame excuses. It's no use saying "I had to try a yoke of oxen". Or "I bought a farm and had to arrange the mortgage". Or "I married a wife, and so could not come on time".

So what comes first, the individual disciple or the community? The individual must sacrifice himself, with Jesus, to create a community that is free to love in a personal and creative way. And then Jesus and the community sacrifice themselves to promote free creative persons. Free to love.

Discussion Questions

Why does Jesus not answer the question directly?

What is attractive about legalism and institutional stuff?

What is a personal commitment to Jesus?

Why can we not follow the crowd?

How do we have to "strive" to get into the kingdom?

Do we have to get through the narrow door on our own?

Why does the door get closed?

What has love got to do with all of this?

Do we make any excuses today, for delaying a personal commitment to Jesus?

Does the individual or the community come first?

22nd Sunday of the year
Invite the blind, the crippled and the lame
Luke 14: 1, 7-14

On this occasion Jesus is having a meal in a Pharisee's house. St Luke implies that Jesus is not as diplomatic as we might expect. He tells the Pharisee that when he is giving a dinner or a lunch, that he should invite the poor, the blind and the lame, rather than his rich friends.

Scripture commentators don't find it easy to explain what is going on here. It is hardly just about going the extra mile for the poor. It is wider than that. Every meal that Jesus celebrates or talks about (whether it is about the Eucharist or not) is what St John in his gospel calls a "sign" that foreshadows, and heralds, a new age that Jesus is making possible. A new age that begins right now. In the new age everybody will have bread on the table. Bread means life, when we have it.

Jesus is not telling the Pharisee here that everybody should become a member of the Christian church. Here Jesus is thinking of the whole human family, including the Pharisee. In the Incarnation, Jesus takes responsibility for the whole human family. Responsibility for the liberation (from every oppressive force), and salvation of the whole human family. He has to begin to establish his reign of justice, freedom and love, not just in the church, but in the human community. The church is a leaven in the human community.

The Pharisees were thinking that the new age would begin with cosmic upheavals in nature and revolutions in the human community. Jesus does not agree with that. Instead, he says that the new age will begin when the blind, the lame and the crippled are invited to dine with the rest of the human family. Jesus seems to have no interest in clean and unclean, secular and profane.

So what? What does that tell us? It tells us that in becoming man (that is, God becoming man), Jesus has changed our self-understanding of what it means to be human. He tells us that every human being has a creative role to play within the human and

Christian communities. It tells us that we are not to be afraid, because Jesus will be present at any meal that we eat with the human family, especially with the poor.

Discussion Questions

All Jesus' meals are a sign of what?

The signs in question foreshadow a new age. What is that today?

What is so special about a meal?

What is the Incarnation?

Jesus has responsibility for the liberation of the human family. What does that mean?

How is Jesus' reign a reign of justice and love?

The church is a leaven within the human community. What does that mean?

What were the Pharisees expecting from the new age?

How has Jesus changed our self-understanding of what it means to be human?

How will Jesus be present at every meal?

23rd Sunday of the year
If a man comes to me without hating his father and mother…
Luke 14: 25-33

"Jesus retained the enthusiasm of the Galilean crowd, but theirs was an uncomprehending enthusiasm" (Caird). They never knew what he was on about! Enthusiasm is important, but it not enough. It is not nearly enough. Without a personal faith and love for Jesus and for his historical mission, he remains a stranger.

Before we start to ask what Jesus means by his demand that we should "hate" our families, we should first understand that we have an emotional commitment to our families, our clans, our tribe, our country, our history, our traditions, our battles, our victories real or imaginary. And then all the propaganda and ideologies that flow from our education systems. We need all these things, but not the bias and the baggage that goes with them. The point is that if we do not put Jesus first, in a personal way, all these family ties get distorted. They'll have us running about like headless chickens!

The cross reminds us of how hostile the human community is to Jesus and his mission and the human community is you and I. "To hate" here is a Semitic exaggeration, coming from the culture of the time. In our time our newspapers exaggerate all the time.

The modern secular city is fiercely competitive. If we are not covered from head to foot in the armour of Christ, the wolves that prowl the secular city, and come into the living room through the television screen, will do themselves an injury laughing!

The secular city is competitive if the individual disciple of Jesus is unable to play a creative role in the human and Christian community, he will be tempted to get his "kicks" in other ways. He will be tempted to compete for the highest seats in the family, the church and the state. He may go chasing after medals and titles. He will be tempted to go back to the crowd, and forget his original dream.

Discussion Questions

Are there any enthusiastic, but uncomprehending, people in the church today?

Why did Jesus say that we should "hate" our families?

Do family ties ever get distorted today?

What does it mean to put Jesus first in a personal way?

How does putting Jesus first, in a personal way, put family ties into focus?

The modern secular city is competitive. What does that mean?

What does it mean to, "Put on the armour of Christ"?

Why do I mention the wolves that prowl the secular city today?

Does the cross suggest that the world is hostile, in some way, to what is human?

24th Sunday of the year
There will be rejoicing in heaven over one repentant sinner
Luke 15: 1-32

"Jesus' critics here are the Scribes and Pharisees. They think that their whole duty is to avoid anything that could contaminate their sanctity. They are bewildered by Jesus' disregard for their spiritual security policy" (Caird). They are horrified that Jesus should eat and drink and celebrate with sinners and low-life of all sorts.

The parable of the Prodigal Son (or the two sons) does not begin with the usual question. "St Luke assumes that the Scribes and Pharisees will recognise how they are being addressed here. The story is more pastoral than historical" (La Verdiere). In other words, St Luke is using the parable to instruct the Christian communities that he is writing for now. The open fellowship of the early church, at the Lord's Table, is being questioned.

St Luke is using the gospel here to speak directly to his communities. In the parable, the younger son is bored with family responsibilities, and goes away on a daft adventure. Somewhat like some young people today who are sometimes tempted by the glamour of the drugs industry.

The Prodigal son ended up feeding pigs for a Gentile master. He was hungry, because he was too disgusted to dine with the pigs! After his experience of hardship with the farmer and the pigs, he was more disposed to see his family in a new light.

The parable reassures members who have become estranged from the community that when they return, they will not be in trouble. The Prodigal's father saw the boy returning from a long way off. The family had to rejoice and kill the fatted calf.

Meanwhile, the negative reaction of the Elder Son is not dramatised. In anger, the Elder Son thinks of himself as his Father's slave, "I have slaved for you". And he calls his brother "This son of yours". The Father refuses to take sides.

We are not told what happens to the Elder Son in the end. But he and the respectable Jews that he represents here are warned that they will be strangers to God unless they are able to rejoice over the restoration of sinners. Jesus gives life! God gives life! Jesus tells us what is involved in Christian love. And that love is not optional.

Discussion Questions

Does this parable suggest that the communities that St Luke is writing for have some problems?

What sort of things might contaminate our sanctity today?!

Why did the prodigal Son leave home?

Why do some young people leave home today?

Did the pigs help the prodigal Son in any way?

What sorts of people does the church find difficult today?

Who does the Elder Son represent today?

Does the Elder Son have a problem?

Why are we not told what happened to the Elder Son in the end?

Is there a warning here for the Elder Sons of the church today?

25th Sunday of the year
The children of this world are more astute in dealing with their own kind, than the children of light
Luke 16: 1-13

What is very different about this parable is that Jesus is talking about a crisis in a purely secular and economic context. And the man in charge is dishonest, as well!

"The manager is about to lose his job on account of his bad reputation. He provides for his future security by manipulating his employer's accounts to the advantage of his employer's debtors. Thereby the debtors are made to incur a debt of gratitude to the unscrupulous manager who has saved them a lot of money. It is expected that the debtors will reward their benefactor later on. Worldly people tend to deal more swiftly and shrewdly with crisis than the less worldly do with crisis of a more profound and ultimate nature. Jesus presented the kingdom of God as a crisis confronting all of mankind, and warning against apathy and inertia in the face of such a crisis" (Fr James Gaffney).

In the old days, the church in Europe often gave the impression, in a very holy and pious way (!) that we should all be resigned to whatever the Lord sends. St Therese of Lisieux (in 1890s France), tells us that the Convent was so cold (she was plagued by chilblains) that she thought that the sisters were tempting Providence! And she was not one to complain about anything!

In this parable, Jesus is telling his disciples that they can learn something from the market-place. The human community today is not resigned to cold, hunger and disease. Not in Europe at any rate. The human community is not fatalistic as it sometimes was in the pre-scientific age. We believe that we can fight, in a creative way, against the limitations that nature imposes upon us (diseases, for example), and the oppressive limitations of human development – lack of freedom, lack of justice and human rights.

If the church can learn something from the unjust steward, it can surely learn something from the many scientific and wise people that are involved in human development today.

The kingdom of justice and love that Jesus is here to establish is a gift, a task and a challenge. The challenge is this: every disciple of Jesus has a mission to work in a creative way with Jesus and the Holy Spirit, and the human community, to rid our world of any and every oppressive force that devalues the human person and the human community.

It is at the heart of the struggle for human liberation and salvation, that we meet Jesus and the Christian God.

Discussion Questions

What was the steward up to here?

Do Christians always use their talents today?

Would it be all right for a disciple of Jesus to be resigned i.e. to take no responsibility for hunger and disease?

If the church failed to promote justice, freedom and human rights, would it bring the church into disrepute?

Can the church learn anything from modern science?

How does the promotion of human rights help to establish the reign of Jesus and God?

Is the kingdom that Jesus is establishing just a miraculous event, or something that we can get involved in bringing about?

Can the Christian and human communities work together in building the kingdom?

26th Sunday of the year
They have Moses and the Prophets
Luke 16: 19-31

Originally, this gospel was directed at the Pharisees. Now St Luke is telling us that there are some Pharisee-type people in the Christian communities that he is writing for.

"There is no suggestion here that the rich man's wealth was ill-gotten, or that Lazarus was a victim of oppression. The rich man's sins consisted not in what he did, but in what he failed to do" (McCarthy).

The really scary part of this parable for us today is that the rich man was a believer in the God of Abraham, Isaac and Jacob. Why did he not allow the Scriptures to guide his life?

We have a childish tendency to think that all we need – as individuals – is a copy of the Bible. And all we have to do is read it. We can do that. But first the gospel has to pass through the community. It is the community that interprets the Scriptures - especially in the television age.

The rich man's first problem was that he allowed himself to be hijacked by the establishment. He just followed the powers that be. The scriptures had no personal or emotional meaning for him. He did not see Lazarus as a person with human and religious rights. Lazarus was just another thing at his gates. The religious establishment, at the time, expected to find salvation mainly in the detailed observance of the Law.

The rich man here belonged to a class of rich men who controlled the market-place. These men (and they were men!) made the rules in favour of themselves and imposed their class culture on the common man and woman. They tended to think that riches were a sign of divine favour. And that poverty was a sign of punishment for sin.

The people in power then begin to believe their own spin-doctors and over time become institutionalised and mechanical in operation. People like Lazarus have no voice. In this parable Lazarus does not speak. They expect the Scriptures to support their prejudices.

Even in Hades, Lazarus is still pontificating and domineering! He wants Abraham to come up with a special revelation for his brothers who are still on earth. In effect, he is trying to make it possible for his brothers to bypass the religious community on earth. And also to bypass the Scriptures that he bypassed while he was on earth!

Of course the Christian church has to have an institutional aspect, but at its deepest level the church still remains a mystery of faith and love.

Discussion Questions

Are riches a sign of divine favour?

Was the rich man's wealth ill-gotten?

Was Lazarus oppressed?

Was it what the rich man failed to do that landed him in Hades?

Did the institutional (impersonal) aspect of his religion take over the rich man's life?

Why did the rich man not see Lazarus as a person with human and religious rights?

The rich man belonged to a class of rich people. Did this make a difference?

Even in Hades the rich man is still giving orders. Is that surprising?

Did the rich man have difficulty in interpreting the Scriptures?

27th Sunday of the year
If only you had faith!
Luke 17: 5-10

The faith in question here is Christian faith. A disciple's faith begins in a way that is (in the world's view) small, like a mustard seed, but has great potential for growth.

The danger for disciples today is that they may want to run in the ways of faith before they have learned to walk. What does that mean? It means that the disciples have to take the humanity of Jesus seriously – and their own humanity. In other words, we cannot bypass the humanity of Jesus and go straight to his divinity. We cannot bypass his humanity which includes his historical life and mission.

The humanity of Jesus includes his historical project or mission, to open the eyes of the blind and set the downtrodden free. Once we begin, with Jesus, to set the downtrodden free, we begin to understand the mystery of what faith in Jesus and his liberating work is all about.

For a disciple there are no flyovers or underpasses to get around the humanity of Jesus. He tells us himself "No one can come to the Father except through me. I've been with you all this time, and you still don't know me. He who sees me sees the Father".

The mystery of faith cannot be separated from the mystery of love. That is why Jesus here talks about the servant who is looking for a reward for the work that he does. In the culture that we live in today, we usually work for a reward or a wage of some kind. St Luke says that a disciple does not work for a reward. Presumably, we can call love a reward.

Why is that? A disciple's relationship to Jesus is not a professional one. There is no contract. There is no nine-to-five job with a guaranteed pension with enhancement! A disciple belongs to Jesus in a personal way. We share his life by faith and love, which helps to explain why it is possible for a disciple to say to a mulberry tree "Be uprooted and planted in the sea".

This faith and love grows by critically listening to the word of Jesus. The word of Jesus does not become fully real for us until the local Christian community makes the word of Jesus its own word. And relates it to what is happening in human history.

Discussion Questions

Why do we have to take the humanity of Jesus seriously?

Why do we have to take our own humanity seriously?

Why not go straight to the divinity of Jesus?

Why does a disciple of Jesus not look for a reward? (Except the reward of love).

Why can the mystery of faith not be separated from the mystery of love?

Does a disciple have a professional contract with Jesus?

What does it mean to belong to Jesus in a personal way?

Faith grows by critically (or personally) listening to the word of Jesus. What does "critically" mean here?

28th Sunday of the year
No one has come back to give praise to God but this foreigner
Luke17: 11-19

Here Jesus meets ten lepers. Leprosy was contagious and incurable at the time. As the disease advanced, it deformed the body. The leper had to live in isolation from the human and religious communities. He was also isolated from his own family.

One of the lepers was a Samaritan. The Samaritans were partly of the Jewish faith and partly pagan. Jews did not speak to Samaritans. On one occasion Jesus was accused of being a Samaritan! The Samaritans had a Sanctuary of their own.

Now Jesus is not interested in random miracles. Nine of the lepers who were cured on this occasion continued as non-believers in Jesus. Jesus wanted to deal a permanent blow to leprosy. He wants to heal more than the leper's skin. He wants to heal the whole person, because this disease wounds and devalues the whole community.

But a person is not fully healed until he or she comes to Jesus in a personal way. He or she has to believe in Jesus. And that includes believing in his historical project to liberate and save the human family. Thus, the healing of the leper anticipates and heralds the dawn of a new age when everybody will be liberated from the oppressive power of disease, and restored to the community.

St Luke says that the Samaritan leper was the only one fully cured and saved on this occasion. He returned to Jesus to thank him personally. And so Jesus can say to the man "Your faith has saved you". To believe in Jesus in a personal way is to believe and get involved in his liberating and saving historical work. To believe in Jesus in a personal way, we have to do more than follow the crowd. Personal belief involves us in personal risk. The other nine lepers may have gone off to play bingo or watch a Soap Opera (!) or gone off to support the abortion industry or whatever.

In any case, we do not become adult believers in Jesus until we get involved in his historical work to heal the sick and set the downtrodden free.

Discussion Questions

Did the leper have an easy life?!

Any leper-type people about today?

Why is Jesus not interested in random miracles?

Why did the other nine not return to thank Jesus?

Did Jesus want to heal the whole person, and not just his skin?

Does Jesus want the lepers to believe in him in a personal way? What is a personal way?

How does the healing of the leper here anticipate the dawn of a new age?

Can we believe in Jesus without taking a personal stand to support his liberating and saving work?

29th Sunday of the year
A God who listens
Luke 18: 1-8

This parable has to do with how God's "chosen ones" can get justice. At the time, the poor lacked the means to bribe the unjust judges. They also lacked influential friends who would support their case. The only weapon that they had was persistent prayer. The judge was afraid that he would be nagged to death if he did not give the widow what she wanted! Now the questions are these: who are the "chosen ones" (or elites), and why do they need to cry to Jesus or God night and day, in prayer?

The chosen ones have responsibility, with Jesus and the Holy Spirit, for evangelising the community. "Election" (i.e. being chosen) might seem a sign of God's favouritism towards his own people, but this is true only in a paradoxical way. Israel came to be known as "God's elect" only in the days of her national humiliation. "The elect are those who are specially called to serve God through suffering for their faith at the hands of an ungodly world" (G. B. Caird).

What is different about the elect (or chosen ones) is that they do not abandon the sheep as soon as they see the wolf i.e. (the oppressor) coming. They do not hide behind the community. They do not take care of their own comfort and privileges first! They put their life on the line to give life; to give life to the poor and the rich too! Their priority has to do with giving life, rather than putting the defence of the community first. "I'm sending you out like lambs among wolves".

The chosen keep the commandments, but they do not tick boxes in a mechanical way. The chosen have to take on a creative and responsible role for rediscovering the mystery of love embodied in the commandments. To do that they have to rediscover Jesus' new commandment first. As Scripture says, they have to be able, with the help of the Holy Spirit, to bring "Things old and new out of the depths of revelation".

The chosen need to pray constantly, because they live in a (human) community that does not always promote justice, freedom and human rights. They also live in a (Christian) community. In the Christian community there will be some people who are afraid to do battle with the wolves that attack the sheep and lack the strength of faith to believe that Jesus will hear their prayers.

St Luke wants to reassure the "chosen ones" that Jesus and God will always hear their prayers. We will never fully believe that, until we try it! But they should not always expect an instant answer. He will answer when the time is right. Meanwhile, he wants us to listen in a creative way to the gospel of Jesus and to persevere in prayer.

Anybody who is human belongs to "the chosen" to a greater or lesser degree. But St Luke's focus in this parable is on the poor and downtrodden.

Discussion Questions:

Is being chosen by Jesus or God a sign of favouritism?
Do Jesus' chosen ones suffer more than others?

Do some shepherds abandon the sheep when they see the wolf coming?

Do the chosen ones tick the communities' boxes in a mechanical way?

What is a creative responsibility for rediscovering the mystery of love embodied in the commandments?

What is Jesus' new commandment?

Why do the chosen ones need to pray constantly?

Is it easy to believe that Jesus or God will always answer prayer?

Is it easy to pray constantly?

30th Sunday of the year
The cries of the poor
Luke 18: 9-14

Not all the Pharisees were like the one in this parable. The Hebrews like to paint pictures in black and white. St Luke is trying to tell the Christian community that Pharisaism is a permanent temptation for Christians.

The Pharisee is not presented as a man who robbed banks (his own or others!). Nor did he beat up his family. "He was scrupulously honest, a faithful family man, and a meticulous observer of the Law. He fasted twice a week. The Law expected him to fast only once a week. He paid tithes on all commodities" (McCarthy).

"Still, Rabbinic literature provides enough parallels to show that Jesus' portrait was no caricature" (Caird). Professor Caird quotes from an old Jewish Prayer book where a Jewish man thanks God that he was not born a slave or a woman!!

St Paul, who was a Pharisee before his conversion, tells us that the old Law can be deadly when separated from Jesus' new law of love because all the commandments get distorted. The individual becomes too professional and mechanical and it makes other people seem not fully real. Jesus deals with the old Law by giving us his own new commandment – that we should love one another, as he has loved us. We need other people to support our all too human efforts, to become more human and Christian.

Once Jesus' new commandment is taken on board, all the other laws and commandments are reoriented. The individual disciple of Jesus and the Christian community has to begin to take personal and creative responsibility for a more personal understanding of all the commandments. Without Jesus' new commandment, all the commandments tend to get distorted.

The Publican in this parable was a human and religious outcast. He collected taxes for the foreign power (the Romans). The tax system made it easy for him to fiddle the tax books. But on this occasion he was able to face the truth about himself. He was a public sinner but he was able to believe that God can and does forgive sinners. He can bring life out of death. "My son was dead and has come back to life" (Lk 15, 24) The Publican could now go home at peace with the community and with God.

Discussion Questions

Does St Luke see a Pharisee lurking within every human being?

Any Pharisee-type people about today?

Why are the Pharisees presented here as morally good?

Why does Jesus give us a new commandment of love?

Does Jesus' new commandment reorientate all the other commandments?

Can the commandments be kept in a mechanical way?

What happens when the commandments get distorted?

Was the Publican a public sinner?

Is it easy to believe that Jesus or God can forgive?

31st Sunday of the year
The Son of Man has come to seek out and save what was lost.
Luke 19: 1-10

"Jericho was a wealthy city. The Romans carried its dates and balsam to world-wide trade and fame. Josephus called it 'A divine region'" (Barkley).

Zacchaeus was a public sinner, a social and religious outcast. He could not go to the market in the daytime. He could not go to the Synagogue at any time. He collected taxes for a foreign power, the Romans, and fiddled the books. He was seen as low life in that culture. Mingling in this crowd was dangerous for him unless he had some disguise. He could have been beaten-up at any time.

St Luke says that as the drama developed, the whole crowd started to complain that Jesus had gone to stay at a sinner's house. What St Luke is saying here is perfectly clear. He is saying that public sinners and religious outcasts can come to Jesus, or that Jesus will come to them – even when some or all the members of the community are hostile.

Like Zacchaeus they must come down from their stupid perches and start to get involved in Jesus' historical project. Zacchaeus gets involved by giving half of his wealth to the poor. Other rich people today can get involved in Jesus' historical project, by producing more bread, better medicine, building schools and hospitals. In the old days we were less aware of how the human community can get involved in Jesus' historical project.

When a person comes to Jesus, he or she goes deeper into the mystery of what it means to be human. What it means to promote justice and peace, freedom and human rights, they can help all of us to get more involved in the adventure of becoming human.

The rich person needs to enter into dialogue with the word of Jesus. The church can help. But Vatican II reminds us that the church does not have ready made social answers. The church's answers have to be forged in dialogue with the human community. (Vatican II The Church Today 16)

Discussion Questions

What is a public sinner? Any about today?

What was a religious outcast?

What was Zacchaeus doing that was wrong?

What is St Luke telling us here? Don't forget that St Luke is evangelising in the Gentile or pagan world.

Any of Zacchaeus' type about today?

How did Jesus help Zacchaeus? And Why?

Why did the rich man promise to give money back?

What do the disciples give to the poor today?

Is Jesus' offer here open to all rich people?

Do riches and power cast a spell on the Christian community today?

Is it difficult for rich man or woman to believe in Jesus?

32nd Sunday of the year
He is the God of the living
Luke 20: 27-38

Here the Sadducees bring a ridiculous question about the resurrection to Jesus. As it is not a serious question, some people will suspect that it is recorded in the gospel because it tells us something about the attitude of the upper classes of Israel, at the time, to Jesus.

"The Sadducees' party was drawn from the top classes of higher officials, wealthy merchants, landowners and priests. It was from their party that statesmen and diplomats were chosen" (McCabe). They were quite happy to collaborate with the Romans, to protect their class and their privileges. The Sadducees believed in unrestricted free will! They did not believe in a personal resurrection. But, in effect, they invented a phoney impersonal resurrection of their own. They said that a man could live on (here on earth) in his descendents. So they came to Jesus with a pointless debate about a woman who had seven husbands. Who would be her husband at the resurrection? They were vaguely hoping that this would weaken belief in the resurrection.

In the parallel account of this gospel (in St Matthew), Jesus says to the Sadducees "You are wrong, because you know neither the Scriptures, nor the power of God". In fact, they only accepted the parts of the Scriptures that fitted their life-style.

Jesus' reply to the Sadducees is hard for us to understand, because it is Rabbinic. Jesus himself told us to look for historical signs of the resurrection. In Moses' time, the Jews were slaves in Egypt. And in Scripture a slave is someone who is described as "dead". Moses brought the community back to life by leading them to freedom in the Promised Land.

Faith in the resurrection is faith in a God who wants to give life to all. But Christian faith requires that we get personally involved. Moses did not sit at home and wait for God to liberate the Jewish people. He had to risk his life by going to the King of Egypt. He had to confront the King with menaces.

The resurrection does not become real for us until we get involved in helping to liberate people from hunger, disease, injustice and so on. Faith in the resurrection does not take us out of the human community. It gives more responsibility for setting the community free.

Discussion Questions

Why were the Sadducees playing games with belief in the resurrection?

Did the Sadducees belief in unrestricted free will have anything to do with their unbelief?

Why did the Sadducees cherry-pick the parts of Scripture that they believed in?

Was their lack of faith related to their class and life-style?

Is the resurrection a miracle that we can observe from a distance?

Moses liberated the slaves. What has that got to do with the resurrection?

Does our helping the poor help us to believe in the resurrection now?

Does faith in the resurrection take us out of the human community?

33rd Sunday of the year
Your endurance will win you your lives
Luke 21: 5-19

Today the church thinks of itself as a Pilgrim People, on a journey with the rest of the human family. In the old days we tended to think of the church as a fortress built on a hill, and having the answer to every question. And nothing to learn!

St Luke is quite clear that Jesus' followers are being maltreated and persecuted from outside. The natural reaction to that is to become defensive. But that is not St Luke's reaction. He says that when the church is persecuted "This will be your opportunity to bear witness" to Jesus and his teaching.

St Luke says that there is no need to be afraid. The disciple who takes the risk of witnessing to Jesus will be assisted by Jesus himself. "He himself will give you an eloquence and a wisdom that none of your opponents will be able to resist or contradict".

This painful time for the community will be made more painful by some of the members of the community who want to live in the past. What form will this deviancy take today? "The greatest temptation of modern man is to escape into a formless sea of irresponsibility, which is the crowd" (Thomas Merton). A Disneyland with Mickey Mouse theology. Where would we be likely to meet it?

A major question for the church today has to do with implementing Vatican II at school and Parish level. Some members will want to implement Vatican II at the local level, while others will be in denial.

The point is that the church finds itself in a very competitive situation today. At school, our children are told that they have to be prepared to compete for work and careers in the modern city. They can seldom expect to follow on the footsteps of their parents as regard work, for example.

This competitive thing also applies in the way that the gospel has to be presented. Children will no longer repeat parrot-fashion anything that the catechism or the teacher says. The children want a creative role in reshaping the catechetical material that they are learning.

Children today know their human and Christian rights. The children want an active part in anything and everything that they are learning.

Discussion Questions

Is the church ever persecuted today?

Should the church be defensive when persecuted?

Is there a risk in witnessing to Jesus today?

Is the church ever persecuted by some of its own members?

Is it difficult to implement Vatican II in the school and the parish today?

Why is the children's education in school competitive today?

Why are children in school encouraged to play an active and creative part in their own education?

Are you happy with the way that the gospel is presented today at parish level?

Should the Laity have a more active role in presenting the gospel today?

Christ the King
The leaders jeered at him
Luke 23: 35-34

We need to remember that St Luke worked with St Paul. He is mostly interested in making the gospel intelligible to the Gentile communities. At the cross, the gentiles are mainly represented by the rulers, the soldiers and the unrepentant thief. The groups in question invite Jesus to come down from the cross. The implication being that there are easier ways to liberate and save the human family.

The rulers and the other hostiles are really afraid of Jesus. Jesus is a homeless Prophet from the despised province of Galilee who has been questioning the established religious order based in Jerusalem. And the established political order based in Rome. Most people then and now want to follow the crowds. They want to work all day, pay the mortgage and watch the soaps in the evening. They do not want to get involved in a critical and personal struggle to build a more human world.

Meanwhile, Jesus cannot work a miracle to save himself. He cannot lay his humanity aside for a little while and take refuge in his divinity! His humanity includes his liberating and saving work, out there at the heart of the human struggle for justice, freedom and love.

Jesus cannot take refuge in his divinity, because the human family has to be liberated and saved in a human way. His solidarity with the struggles of the human family is personal and total. He gives everything. Including his blood.

Most Kings and Rulers tend to use force and violence to promote their communities. To a large extent this is escapism. They are looking for instant mechanical answers to something that should only be approached in a human and personal way.

Christians today will be tempted to focus on the divinity of Jesus to avoid the challenging questions of justice and love that his life and mission raise for us.

We cannot really accept the humanity of Jesus without somehow getting involved in his historical struggle for justice and peace. It is when we ourselves get involve in Jesus' critical struggle for justice, freedom and love, that we begin to understand what kind of King Jesus was in his time and continues to be today.

"In today's world, a strong faith can only develop within the public square, in a challenging debate and dialogue with the realities of life and progress" (Archbishop Diarmuid Martin).

Discussion Questions

Why did the rulers and soldiers mock Jesus?

Who did the rulers and soldiers represent?

Are the rulers and soldiers afraid of what Jesus stands for?

Who would be likely to be afraid of Jesus today?

Why do they ask Jesus to come down from the cross?

Was Jesus wise to question the established religious order?

Was Jesus wise to question the established political order?

Why are most people happy to follow the crowds?

Do many Christians today feel responsible for the liberation of the human community?

What was the driving force behind the human life of Jesus?

Saints Peter and Paul, Apostles
I will give you the keys of the kingdom
Matthew 16: 13-19

Peter's mission has to do with the unity of the church, as it prepares for its world-wide mission to establish Jesus' kingdom of justice and love. Peter has the keys "To the kingdom" because the establishment of the kingdom is the church's priority. The church's priority is not to take care of itself!

The church will be built on Peter, the Rock, but Jesus reminds Peter that the church remains Jesus' church ("I will build my church"). Why the reminder? Because when the barque of Peter runs into heavy seas in the world, Peter will be tempted to take over! Indeed, right there in the gospel, Peter advises Jesus that Jerusalem was too dangerous a place for Jesus to go. Peter was not inclined to take risks for the kingdom on that occasion. Jesus said to Peter "Get behind me, Satan" (Mt. 16, 22). Peter is aware of his weakness and sinfulness when he denies Jesus three times. This is not an obstacle to Peter's mission because he knows that he is a sinner, and is ready to repent.

St Paul's mission has to do with what he calls "The unsearchable riches of Christ". But first St Paul wants to say that the Jews and Gentiles now form one human and religious community. The wall that separated Jews and Gentiles has been pulled down by the death and resurrection of Jesus. Now the whole human family takes its life and mission from Jesus Christ.

Strange to say, St Paul has to go back to original sin to help him to establish the mysterious unity of the human family. And God's mysterious plan to liberate and save the human family. Original sin is a mysterious sin of the human race. He says that all have sinned, Jews as well as Gentiles. And they have all been set free by the death and resurrection of Jesus. St Paul is well aware of individual personal sin, but his priority has to do with unmasking the original sin of the race. Structural sin. We have difficulty in understanding what St Paul is talking about, because we are concentrated on our individual sin and salvation.

St Paul says that we should stop worrying about ourselves, and get involved in the struggle to liberate and save other people.

Discussion Questions

What are the keys that St Peter has?

What are the gates of the underworld?

Where could we see the gates of the underworld today?

What kind of Rock is Peter?

What do we think of Peter's weaknesses?

Why does St Paul focus on the mystery of Christ?

Why does St. Paul want to bring the Jews and Gentiles into one community?

What is original sin? Is it mysterious?

What are St Paul's "Unsearchable riches of Christ?"

What is the unity of the church?

The Assumption
He has exalted the lowly
Luke 1: 39-56

St Luke tells us that Mary travelled from Nazareth to visit Elizabeth. "In Mary the New Testament reaches out to the Old, and transforms it, and gives it its ultimate significance" (LaVerdiere).

So what does Mary bring to the transformation of the Old Testament? Does she bring a more complicated system of law? No. does she bring a new military vision? No. Or a new political vision? We'll leave that question for now.

Mary and the New Testament bring a more human and personal way of life. This is founded on Jesus, who is a perfect human being. He has a mother and a grandmother. But Mary brings more than this. She also brings her personal belief in Jesus, the word made flesh. She also believes in his liberating and saving historical mission, within the historical pilgrimage of the human family.

In the Magnificat, St Luke unveils something of Mary's personal belief in the life and mission of Jesus: "He pulls down the mighty from their seats and exalts the lowly". And then by mentioning the Promise to Abraham, he witnesses to her faith in the history of salvation.

So why does the church need to highlight the significance of Mary and the humanity of Jesus for today? The short answer is that we live in a scientific culture. Some readers will be inclined to say "So what? What has science got to do with the way that Christians express their faith today?" Well, the Old Testament Psalmist tells us that "The heavens declare the glory of God". No doubt. But it is harder, a lot harder, to believe that today. Why? Modern science is able to explain what is going on in the heavens. It has to a large extent removed the mystery and the sacred aspect from the heavens. It is very difficult to "worship" (if that is the right way of expressing it!) what we control. I suspect that it would be harder to see the moon as a romantic object, after the astronauts have danced a jig on the surface of the moon!

But be that as it may, what is very clear is that if somebody failed to believe in God in the middle ages, the human community would tend to think of him as weird, because the culture, at the time, was religious and sacred. In our scientific culture people tend to go in the opposite direction. A lot of people are inclined to think that somebody who believes in God today is weird! I'm talking about the wider human community only of course.

But for Christians, and for many members of the ordinary human community, the glory of God is still visible! It is to be found in the human person and the human and Christian communities. From a scientific viewpoint, the heavens are less mysterious, but the human and Christian communities are more mysterious!

For what its worth, my own feeling is that the heavens can still "Declare the glory of God", provided that we approach the heavens as believers. That is, from within the mystery of the Incarnation and the human community. In other words, Jesus himself has to show us how to read the heavens today.

Discussion Questions

What does Mary bring to the transformation of the Old Testament?

Jesus has a mother and a grandmother. What does that tell us?

Mary believes in Jesus' historical mission. What mission is that?

Jesus exalts the lowly. How does that help the community to develop?

Do the heavens proclaim the glory of God today?

Has science removed something of the mystery and the sacred from the heavens?

Is the moon a romantic object today?

Why do some people today think that it's weird to believe in God?

Where is the obvious place to find the sacred today?

All Saints
Blessed are the poor in spirit
Matthew 5: 1-12

When we think of the Saints today, we tend to think of them as people living in Convents and Monasteries. We think of them as people who are passive and resigned to the unjust forces that often stalk the secular city, and sometimes stalk the Christian church.

This spirituality has passed its sell-by date. Children in Catholic schools today are being educated to fight their Christian corner in the secular city. They are educated to compete and battle for justice, freedom and human rights. The Parish community cannot turn a blind eye to what is happening in our schools. As the Archbishop of Dublin (Diarmuid Martin) said recently, "Faith must be nurtured and protected within real life. In today's world, a strong faith can only develop within the public square, in a challenging debate and dialogue with the realities of life and progress".

This new spirituality (social as well as personal) needs to be taken on board by the Parish community. Why it that? Because many Catholics today are still "cradle Catholics". They come to the church with their family. Seldom do they go through a conversion experience that brings them face to face with the person of Jesus and his plan for the liberation and salvation of the human family. St Paul says that before a disciple gets involved in the secular city, he or she needs the "Shield of faith" and "The sword of the Spirit". The "Sword of the Spirit" is of course the word of Jesus. Where can a disciple acquire this sword today? How can we get down to the mysterious depths of what Jesus is saying to us today?

The sword will not be handed to us today without a fight. "The Kingdom of heaven is like a treasure hidden in a field. When a man discovers it, he sells all that he has and buys the field". I know we all have copies of the gospel these days. So why can't we use them? We can use them, but the gospel does not come alive for us, not fully alive anyway, until it passes through the humanity of the local Christian community. The local Christian community has to make the word of

Jesus its own word. No disciple can do this on his or her own. Why not? Because no individual (including the priest) has all the gifts of the Holy Spirit (the Spirit of Jesus). It is the community that has all the gifts of the Spirit. It is when these gifts are shared that the community is able to get down into the depths, the mysterious depths, of the word of Jesus. This will not happen in an adult way until individual members of the Community come together to listen to the word of Jesus and begin to relate his liberating and saving word to the modern world, and their own lives. This has to be done in small Base communities.

Pope Paul V1 described the Base community as "A hope for the universal Church".

Discussion Questions

St Luke has to interpret the gospel for the gentiles. Do we have to do any interpreting to do?

Should Christians be resigned to social injustice today?

Are our children educated to compete and battle for justice today?

"A strong faith can only develop within the public square". Do we agree?

What is a cradle Catholic?

What is involved in conversion to the faith?

What is "The sword of the Spirit"?

Why does a disciple have to sell all to acquire the treasure hidden in the field?